Manual of Wigmaking

Manual of Wigmaking

MARY BOTHAM
Hairdressing and Boardwork Tutor,
Stockport College for Further Education

and

L. SHARRAD, M.I.T.
Head of Hairdressing Department,
Hollings College (formerly The Domestic and Trades College),
Manchester

Illustrations by

JAMES HARDAKER and WILMAR BAILEY

HEINEMANN : LONDON

William Heinemann Ltd

LONDON MELBOURNE TORONTO

CAPE TOWN AUCKLAND

First published 1964
Reprinted 1965

© Mary Botham and L. Sharrad 1964

Printed and bound in Great Britain
by Bookprint Limited, Kingswood and Crawley

Foreword

by A. Churchill

I must congratulate Mrs Botham and Mr Sharrad on their wonderful effort in putting such a manual on record. As a very old boardworker and posticheur, and having won National and International awards and prizes of honour, including being the first winner of the Gold Cup 1929, I know this subject is most difficult to elucidate.

To anyone wishing to become a real craftsman I can strongly recommend this book for study, but one also needs plenty of patience and practice and, if possible, guidance from one skilled in the art. There is no doubt that when one can claim to know boardwork and postiche, one really has reached the top in the hairdressing profession because this is the real art of the craft; in fact, salon work by comparison is relatively easy!

A.C.

v

Preface

This book has been written in response to the need for a detailed explanation of the many and varied processes involved in the art and craft of boardwork. It also covers the syllabuses required for the City and Guilds of London Institute's examinations in Hairdressing.

Hitherto, the passing on of skills in this subject has depended largely on practical demonstration supplemented by the teacher's notes. Inevitably then, much teaching time has been spent in note-taking, with its attendant evils of boredom and loss of interest. Perhaps, too, as a further result some of the techniques have developed inaccuracies.

The authors would not suggest that only the methods referred to in this book are acceptable. Neither would they wish to give the impression that every facet of the art of wig-making has been covered. They do hope, however, that a sound basis has been offered to all those who are engaged in either the teaching or learning of this long-neglected art.

Their grateful thanks are due to James Hardaker and Wilmar Bailey for the meticulous care and tremendous enthusiasm which have been displayed in the preparation of the diagrams.

M.B.
L.S.

Contents

PART I

Postiche Made of Weft

1 BOARDWORK

ORIGIN AND USE

Boardwork is the art of working with hair to make any kind of postiche, from a simple pin-curl to a complete wig. The person who does this work is called a boardworker because he or she works at the board or bench.

Postiche is the name given to a finished piece of hairwork. The person who designs it and does the final dressing out is called a posticheur. Most posticheurs are top-class hairdressers. The boardworker may not be able to dress hair at all and his work may be confined solely to making postiche of various kinds.

Wigs have been made and worn for various reasons since the earliest times. They are mentioned in many books about the great Chinese, Egyptian, Greek, and Roman civilizations. In Greece it appears that wigs were worn by both men and women and were also used in the theatre. References show that wigs were in use in the early days of the Roman empire; women had wigs of different colours as part of their wardrobe.

France, always a leader of fashion, introduced the peruke in the early seventeenth century and the fashion of wearing wigs as a distinctive feature of dress spread through Europe.

A study of the many famous historical coiffures shows that postiche was widely used in England. As well as the very elaborate styles worn by the élite plain wigs were used by the ordinary person. Some of these wigs were very crudely made and the wigmaker was not very well paid for his labours. This is shown in many seventeenth- and eighteenth-century books and particularly in diaries of this period, where many references to wigs are found. In some eighteenth-century engravings of ancient homes, it is possible to distinguish one or more wig stands in the hall. These look like a wooden block mounted on a base. One can assume that they were used mainly by men, who removed their wigs when visiting in the same way that they remove their hats nowadays.

Members of the legal profession wear wigs as a mark of office. These wigs are made by a separate branch of workers who are not connected with the general hairdressing profession.

Postiche is particularly useful in theatrical and film work, to give the illusion of a change of age, sex, or character. Although the making of theatrical postiche is usually undertaken by theatrical costumiers, the local hairdresser may be asked for help in dressing out wigs for local amateur dramatic productions.

Boardwork is of particular value to people who have become bald or have suffered severe loss of hair through illness or accident, and who may need to wear a complete wig or a small piece of postiche.

A knowledge of boardwork is undoubtedly of help to all hairdressers. Handling, mixing, and matching hair, and an appreciation of colour, quality, and texture are things which aid the hairdresser in the course of his profession. The whole art of wigmaking offers a fascinating study both in theory and practice.

SOURCES AND VARIETIES OF HAIR

Human hair for use in boardwork is obtained either in the form of cuttings or combings, the main source being cuttings.

The best quality cut hair comes from Europe and is in great demand throughout the world. Hair in a virgin state, that is, hair which has not been dyed, bleached, permanently waved, or otherwise treated with chemicals, is usually of the best quality and this is bought mainly from the peasants of various countries. For example, the best quality dark hair comes from Spain, and northern Italy, particularly from Tuscany, while brown and auburn hair is obtained from France. The best blonde hair comes from Germany.

The hair is bought in the first instance by people called hair collectors, who travel over the continent and buy hair. These collectors then sell the hair to the large wholesale houses who prepare it for use. The price of hair varies tremendously according to colour, quality, and texture.

Cheaper grades of hair are obtained from other countries: cheap dark hair comes mainly from China and Japan and is of a coarser texture than European hair.

Hair from the age group 25 to 35 is usually of the best quality because it is then mature in colour and has not begun to turn grey. Children's hair is of little use for wigmaking because it is of varied shades and does not hold a wave or curl well.

Natural white and blonde hair are the most expensive because these are the most difficult to obtain. The best white hair comes from the countries which supply the best dark hair, as dark hair goes a truer white than blonde hair. For making wigs which have to be worn regularly, there is no satisfactory substitute for human hair. Nowadays, nylon hair, which is cheaper, easy to obtain, and can be made in any colour and dressed in any style, is being used, but mainly for theatrical work and window displays—it can look extremely spectacular. For normal wear, however, it has a big disadvantage because it is difficult to restyle. Another drawback is that it is considered unhealthy: nylon hair is non-absorbent and perspiration may cause extreme discomfort to the wearer.

For competition work, wigs or added postiche are often made of mohair, which is fine white long hair, obtained from the Angora goat. It dresses out well and takes colour in the same way as bleached hair but, as it is too soft in texture, it is also unsuitable for regular wear. Another substitute is hair from the yak, a species of ox found in Tibet. This animal, covered all over with a long, thick, silky coat which hangs down almost to the ground, provides hair that can be used in wigmaking.

TOOLS AND MATERIALS USED IN BOARDWORK

Work-bench

A good strong bench or table for working upon, in a good light, is an essential part of any workroom.

Hackle

A series of metal prongs set obliquely in a wooden base and used for disentangling hair. It is usually screwed or clamped to the work-bench [*Figure* 1].

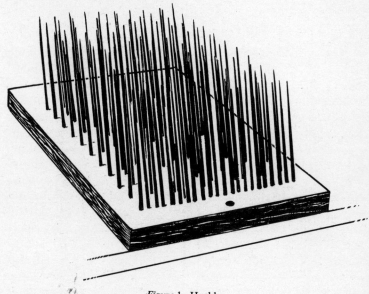

Figure 1. Hackle

Weaving sticks

Two sticks about 10 in. long: the left-hand stick is plain and has a nail for holding the weaving silks; the right-hand one has three grooves on which to wind the weaving silk. These are shaped to fit into —

Wooden clamps or screws

These screw on to the bench and each has a hole of the correct size for holding the weaving sticks. They are used together to make the weaving frame [*Figure* 2].

Drawing brushes

There are two kinds: one is made of wood and set with bristles;

the other has a leather base set with steel pins. Used in pairs, one on top of the other, either kind is employed for holding hair [*Figure* 3].

Jockey

Made of watch-spring, a jockey is used to hold weft in place while weaving.

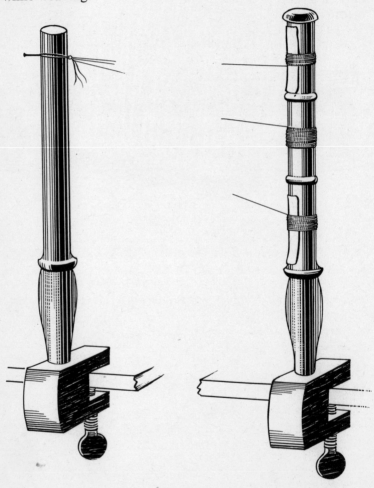

Figure 2. Weaving sticks and clamps

Pressing or pinching irons

These are used for pressing hairwork at various stages of manufacture [*Figure* 4]. If the flat metal disc is used for pressing, it is being used as a pressing iron. If hairwork is placed between the two flat discs it is being used as a pinching iron. There is also a solid metal iron, usually a rectangular shape about 3 in. × 2 in. × 1 in. attached to a handle which can only be used as a pressing iron. Either kind of iron is heated before use.

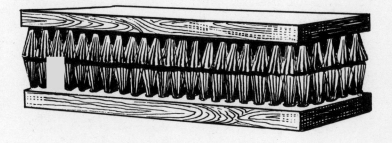

Figure 3. Drawing brushes

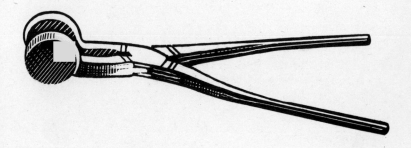

Figure 4. Pinching or pressing irons

Twisting machine

This is a small winding machine threaded with tail cord, it screws on to the bench and is used for winding the stems of switches and pin-curls [*Figure* 5].

Jigger

It is a block of wood 8 in. × 3 in. screwed to the work-bench but with 3 in. projecting [*Figure* 6(1)]. Through this projecting portion, two holes are bored. Strong string is threaded through these and tied to form a loop which hangs down to about 2 in. from the floor. It is used when permanently curling hair on wooden curlers or *bigoudis* [*Figure* 6(2)].

Malleable or soft block

This is made of canvas and stuffed with sawdust and has the approximate shape of a human head. Pins may be pushed into it and it is used for dressing out postiche and knotting the under-side of hairwork. It is made in various sizes from 18 in. to 24 in. in circumference.

Wooden block

It is similar to a malleable block in shape but made of *wood*. Also made in various sizes, it is used for mounting the foundation of wigs, transformations, or smaller pieces of hairwork that are made on a net foundation.

Finger shield

Made of metal, it is shaped like a tube with one slanting end, and is large enough to fit on to the tip of the finger. It is used for picking up the point of the needle when the sewing is done on a wooden block [*Figure* 7].

Knotting hook-holder

This is a steel holder, pencil-shaped, with an adjustable top to hold the knotting or parting hooks used in wigmaking.

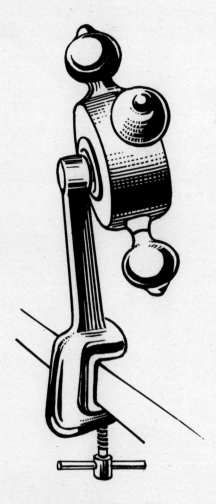

Figure 5. Twisting machine

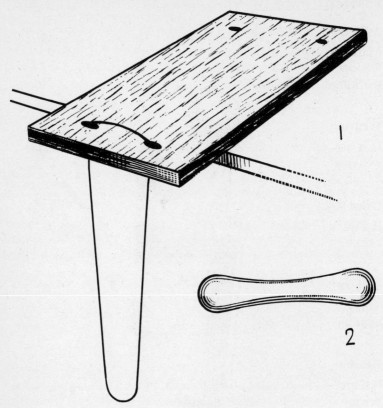

1

2

Figure 6. (1) Jigger, (2) bigoudi

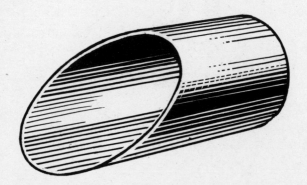

Figure 7. Finger shield

Adjustable block-holder

Made of metal, it screws on to the bench and will hold a wooden or malleable block in any desired position while working.

Weaving silk

Is a strong fine silk, usually purple in colour used on the weaving sticks when weaving hair into weft.

Oiled silk

Is a waterproof silk used on men's postiche to prevent adhesive coming through on to the foundation.

Tail cord

This is a strong waxed cord used on the twisting machine when winding up switches.

Beeswax

A secretion of the honey bee, it is used in boardwork to prevent sewing silk from twisting while working, and to preserve and strengthen both sewing and weaving silk.

Foundation net

This is a fine stiffened silk net used for most foundational postiche. It is made in all shades of brown, blonde, grey, black, and white [see *Figure* 8(4)].

Caul net

A much coarser net, as in *Figure* 8(2), shaped for the crown of the head and used on this portion of a wig only.

Wig net

A type of net similar to caul net but available by the yard. It is usually about 12 in. in width. Both nets are available in colours to match most hair colours [*Figure* 8(3)].

Knotting gauze

A different type of silk net, not stiffened and very light in weight, used for men's postiche and for knotted partings [*Figure* 8(1)].

Parting silk

A very closely-woven strong silk made in white and flesh colour. It is used for making drawn-through partings.

Galloon

This is a very fine strong silk ribbon made in widths from $\frac{1}{4}$ centimetre to $1\frac{1}{2}$ centimetres. It is available in various colours to match foundation net.

Watch spring

Used for making positional springs to hold the main points of wigs and other postiche close to the head.

Fish skin

Is used to cover the tips of the springs or, in the case of white wigs, the entire spring to prevent moisture from the scalp causing the spring to rust and discolour the light-coloured galloon.

Tension springs

Made of fine coiled wire, these are fixed at the nape of the neck to tighten the wig and hold it securely in place on the head.

Block points

These are steel pins, used for pointing or attaching net, galloon, or material to a wooden block.

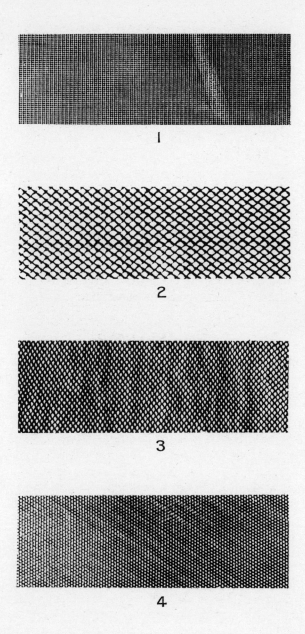

I

2

3

4

Figure 8. Types of net: (1) gauze; (2) caul net; (3) wig net; (4) foundation net.

2 PREPARATION OF HAIR

The preparation of hair covers a number of processes. It is necessary to know all of them, although some are not often performed. The processes include:
1 The preparation of combings and cuttings.
2 Cleansing and disinfecting hair.
3 Methods of preparing curled and waved hair.
4 Mixing, matching, and drawing-off hair.

COMBINGS

Combings are the hairs which fall out naturally when they have finished their life cycle. The normal life of a hair may be anything from three to seven years, although some illnesses cause hair to be shed prematurely.

When long hair was fashionable, it was customary for women to save these combings and have them made up into switches. Cut hair used to be exceedingly scarce and apart from imported hair, or hair bought from convents, combings were extensively used. When hair is mainly worn short, there is not much point in saving combings but reasonably long ones do sometimes come to hand.

At the root, each hair has a tiny white blob which is clearly visible and is known as the bulb of the hair. This is not present on cut hair. The outer layer of hair is composed of overlapping scales arranged in much the same way as the scales on a fish. They are of course extremely tiny. If you run your finger and thumb fairly rapidly down a few long hairs from roots to points, it will travel quite smoothly; but if you try to do so from the points to the roots, it will feel rough. If hair was made up into postiche with the roots and points all mixed up, the hairs would rub against each other and become very tangled and difficult to comb out.

All hair used for wigmaking must be made up so that it lies in the natural direction of the hair growth, and the actual process of sorting out the roots and the points is known as *Turning*. To prepare the hair for turning use the following method:

1 Loosening or teasing

Take a small section of the hair to be turned and shake out any loose dust or foreign matter. Then pull the hair gently apart with the fingers until it is loosened. Treat the whole quantity of hair in this way, making a large pile of loosened hair.

2 Hackling or carding

Fit a hackle firmly to the bench [see *Figure* 1]. Take a handful of the loosened hair and pull one side carefully through the teeth of the hackle. When it is straightened out, turn the section round and straighten out the other half. Lay the straightened hair on the bench. Take hold of the remaining hair in the hackle and continue hackling, first one side and then the other until it is all straightened. Continue taking handfuls of loosened hair until the whole bulk of hair is straightened.

3 Drawing off—level, square, or clubbed

Place all the hackled hair in the drawing brushes and proceed to draw off level at one end. This is done by drawing out fine sections of hair and placing them level in the left hand. Draw off either with the finger and thumb or with the blunt blade of a pocket knife. Do not try to draw out too much hair at once.

When too much hair has been drawn off to hold easily in the left hand, lay it on the bench with the level end to the edge. Continue until all the hair is drawn off. The roots and points are still mixed up but it is now straightened and levelled at one end.

4 Drawing off in lengths

Put the level end of the hair in the brushes and draw off a small section (about as thick as a lead pencil), and make sure that the end is really level. Tie this section with fine string about 3 in. from the level end. This section will be the longest hair. Draw off another section and tie it in the same way. This hair will be slightly shorter. Continue drawing off sections of hair until all the hair down to 3 in. in length is tied in sections ready for turning. Any hair shorter than 3 in. can be discarded.

TURNING

Stage (i)

The most satisfactory method is to prepare a bowl of hot soapy water. Treat each section of hair separately. Hold by the tie and swish the level end vigorously to and fro in the soapy water. This will cause the points of the hair to run back but the roots will remain forward. To make this more pronounced, place the section of hair on the side of the bowl and rub up and down with the finger, half way between the tie and the clubbed end. When the points have all run back, carefully wash the other end of the hair, washing from the tie to the ends of the hair. Try not to entangle this half of the hair.

Rinse the whole section in another bowl of clean water, taking care not to disturb the position of the roots and points. Squeeze out the surplus moisture and put the section of hair on a clean towel. Treat all the sections of hair in the same way and if time permits, allow them to dry. This is really essential if the hair is longer than 8 in. because wet hair stretches so much that it would make the next part of the operation more difficult.

Stage (ii)

Be sure that the hackle is clean, and clear of mixed up hair. Take one section of the turned hair and lightly hackle the unturned end. Turn it round and place a pocket-comb between the points which have run back, and the roots. (With genuine combings it is easy to see which are the roots because the small white blob at the root end is clearly visible.)

Put the comb behind the first row of teeth in the hackle so that the roots are facing you. Draw off the roots only, and, to see that they lie correctly, test the hair by rubbing the points with the finger and thumb: the points should all run back. Place the hair on the bench with the roots pointing to the edge.

The remaining half-section of hair in the hackle should have all the points facing you. Take it out, hackle and reverse it. Again, test by rubbing the points and then place it on the bench with the first half-section of hair, taking care to put the roots the same way — to the edge of the bench.

Stage (iii)

Treat all the sections in the same way. Keep the lengths together: short, medium, and long. Finally, place each length in turn in the drawing brushes and draw off level at the roots. Tie the hair 1 in. from the level end and store until required.

Combings can often be used for making into switches and other postiche and there is no better way of becoming used to handling hair, than to turn a large quantity of combings.

CUTTINGS

Cuttings are hair which has been cut from the head, usually when a client has long hair and wishes to change the style to short hair. If cut hair has been carefully handled it should not require turning but it is always wise to make sure that the hair is not mixed up, by rubbing the ends between the finger and thumb to see that they all run back and are therefore points. If not, they must be turned in the same way as described for combings.

To prepare, cut hair must be cleaned, sterilized, examined to see that there are no nits adhering to it, and drawn off into lengths. If you are dealing with more than one head of hair, try to keep textures, lengths, and colours together: to sort colours, daylight, preferably a northern light, is essential. Divide the hair into suitably sized sections for washing and drying.

Hackle out the very short hair, under 3 in., then club each section and tie securely but not too tightly, so that the string can be moved a little when washing the hair. Prepare a bowl of hot soapy water using either soft soap, shampoo or a detergent, and a small quantity of disinfectant.

Take the sections one at a time and work about in the hot water, allowing it to run down the length from the roots to the points. Do not rub the ends too much, or they will become tangled, particularly the root ends. Slide the tie along so that all the hair can be cleaned thoroughly. If the hair is very greasy or dirty it may require a second washing and this should be done in the same way. When all the sections have been washed, rinse them in clean water, two or three times, until all the soap is removed.

Put the sections of hair on a dry towel and squeeze out the surplus moisture, rolling the hair in the towel and taking care to keep it straight. Allow them to dry either in the open air or in the postiche oven. By drying it in an oven of 80° to 100° centigrade the hair is also sterilized as the heat would destroy any infection which might still be present. When dry, each section should be hackled, drawn off and tied up, after drawing into lengths.

To draw hair into lengths place the level root end in the brushes and draw off all the hair, level at the points. Put the level points in the brushes and draw off the longest hair first, then the medium hair and finally the short hair. Each length will now be clubbed at the root end and should be tied up as the work proceeds. It is usual to store hair clubbed and tied up at the roots.

METHODS OF CLEANSING AND DISINFECTING

Before any hair can be used in boardwork it has to be cleansed and disinfected. It is important that nothing is used on the hair which would impair its elasticity or colour. The instructions given for dealing with a small quantity of cuttings are equally applicable to larger quantities of hair.

As human or animal hair can carry infection it is essential that all hair is thoroughly washed in soap and water and disinfected either by heat, or chemically with a reagent such as formaldehyde, hot carbonate of soda solution, denatured alcohol, or a solution of chlorhexidine which is obtainable in several proprietary preparations. The most common types of bacteria which might be present are those which could cause skin infections. In addition to these, it is necessary to ensure that no nits – the eggs of the *pediculus capitis* (louse) – are adhering to the hair and, if they are, to deal with them as follows.

Nits adhere very firmly to the hair shaft and are not easy to detach. To help the process of removing them, the hair may be boiled in water to which a small amount of acetic acid has been added. Then use a hair 'nitting' machine, which is fixed to the work-bench in front of the hackle. The machine comprises two fine sets of steel teeth which are adjustable to the coarseness of the hair and, by fixing it in front of the hackle, the hair may be drawn through the hackle and the teeth of the nitting machine in one operation. If the hair is drawn through from roots to points the eggs will slide off more easily, as they are usually attached to the hair with the narrow end towards the root. The structure of the hair itself, also affects the removal of the nits.

Any hair containing nits should have a small amount of gammexane, which is a very powerful insecticide, added to the water when being washed.

When the process is complete the hair should be rinsed, dried, and drawn off into lengths before being tied up for storing: as mentioned earlier, hair should be completely dry and always stored where moisture cannot reach it.

Disinfect the hackle and nitting machine before using them for other hair.

PREPARING CURLED OR WAVED HAIR
PERMANENT METHODS

There are three methods of permanently curling hair for use in boardwork:

1 *Frisure forcée*, used for curling or waving hair 6 in. and over in length.
2 Crop curl, used to give a curl to short hair of 3 in. to 5 in.
3 Creoling, used to give a crimp to long hair.

All methods of permanently curling hair are done before the hair is made into postiche. In each case the curl is made permanent by boiling and baking the hair after it has been wound into curls.

1 Frisure forcée

A jigger and wooden curlers called *bigoudis* [*Figure* 6(2)] are used for curling hair by this method. Place the hair in the drawing brushes. Then draw off a small section of hair and tie it ½ in. from the root end with a 10 in. length of string, leaving the long ends for a future purpose. Draw off all the hair and tie in sections. Take one section of hair and place the tied end under the string on the top of the jigger [*Figure* 6(1)] and press down the long loop with the foot. This section of hair will now be held as though it were in a vice.

Take a curler and a piece of end-curl paper and moisten the hair, place the extreme ends in the end paper, take the curler and roll up evenly and tightly: to wind evenly, spread the hair on the curler while winding. Tie the curl securely with the long ends of string which were left for this purpose. After all the curls are rolled up they should be boiled in a pan of water for 15 to 60 minutes, according to the tightness of the curl required and taking into consideration the texture of the hair. Coarse hair will often curl more quickly than fine hair. Afterwards drain and bake the curls in a warm postiche oven for at least 24 hours or until thoroughly dry. The hair is then unwound and tied into bunches.

When curling long hair, it is sometimes advisable to use the spiral method of winding instead of the point-to-root (*croquignole*) method. To do this, after sectioning the hair, tie the root end tightly to one end of the curler and wind the hair smoothly down, advancing slightly with each turn. Finish the ends with end-curl paper or crêpe-hair and tie with string. This method of winding will give a tighter curl down the length of the hair. Boil and bake as before; and when the hair is thoroughly dry, unwind and tie five or six curls together. Comb into waves or curls to store.

2 Crop curl

Place the hair in the brushes. Draw off a small section, moisten the ends, and rub on the palm of the hand. This will 'felt' or mat the ends together and make tying unnecessary. Wet the whole section of hair in water to which a few drops of acetic acid may be added to make the hair more supple and therefore easy to wind. The piece of hair is then wound round a curler, or even a lead pencil. Slide off the hair in the form of a small pin-curl and place it on a wire tray. Put a small weight on the curl to prevent it from coming undone, or a clip could be used. When a tray-full has been prepared, place this over a saucepan half-full of boiling water and steam the curls for 15 to 20 minutes. After steaming, allow it to cool off and then put the tray of curls in the postiche oven to bake. Let the curls cool before storing them away for future use.

3 Creoling

Long hair for making into switches, can be given a permanent crimp by plaiting in fine plaits, tying each end, and boiling and baking. This will give hair the added bulk that is neces sary for a switch, if it is to make a reasonably sized chignon.

NON-PERMANENT METHODS

There are three non-permanent methods of curling or waving hair, all of which are used on finished hairwork where a quick wave or curl is required. They are:
  1 Curling by the paper and pinching method.
  2 Marcel waving.
  3 The box-iron method (obsolete).
All the methods involve the use of heated irons of different kinds.

1 Curling by the paper and pinching method

For this method take a small section of hair, damp it slightly and wind it round a curler. Slip it off in the form of a pin-curl and place it in the centre of a small triangular piece of tissue paper. Keep the curl a good shape, fold over each side of the paper and screw up at the corners to hold the curl in place. These paper screws are called *papillotes*. Prepare all the hair in curls. Heat the pinching irons and press each curl between the flat discs at the end, keeping the curls flat and round. Allow the curls to cool, take off the curl-papers, and the hair may be dressed out as required.

2 Marcel waving

All hairdressers are familiar with this method which involves the use of a special iron, called a marcel waving iron. To wave the hair, heat the iron and with the aid of a comb, manipulate the hair around it to form waves and curls. This form was invented by a young French hairdresser, M. Marcel, in about 1872 but the secret of his discovery was closely guarded until almost the end of the century when he made his methods known generally to the hairdressing world; it was universally acclaimed and adopted as the chief method of waving hair until the advent of permanent waving.

3 The box-iron method

This is an old-fashioned way of crimping hair. The box-iron is like three or four small curling irons joined together with one handle. It is heated and pressed at intervals down the lengths of hair. The result is a series of crimps which would not find much favour in modern hairdressing; during the Victorian era it was used mainly to crimp the front hair which showed beneath the lace caps worn at that time.

MIXING HAIR

It seldom happens that the posticheur has hair of every colour, length, and texture in stock and it is often necessary to mix hair to match a particular pattern. There are three reasons for mixing hair:

1 To obtain a basic shade by mixing two or more colours together.
2 To produce grey hair by adding white to the basic shade.
3 To make tapered hair by mixing various lengths together.
The method for mixing hair is as follows:
Fix the hackle firmly to the bench. Take the two amounts of hair to be mixed and draw together through the hackle until about 4 in. of hair protrudes. Hold this in the left hand and with the first finger of the right hand mix the hair together with a kneading movement — then draw the hair right through. Turn it round and draw the roots also through the hackle. This must be done repeatedly until a perfect mix is obtained.

It is not often that a pattern can be matched by a simple two-colour mixing and it is necessary to study the hair carefully to see which shades go to make up the pattern and to be able to recognize these shades. For example, if a brown shade is required, ascertain whether the basic brown has a yellow or red tone. Sometimes red will need to be added, sometimes yellow.

No head of hair in a natural state is of an even shade all over and this must be carefully observed in wigmaking. The front hair is generally lighter and brighter than the back hair, while grey hair may be present on the temples only. It is therefore important to take patterns of hair from the front, sides, and back when making a full transformation or wig as three different shades may be required. In mixing grey hair the basic shade must be ascertained and mixed, and the amount of white added to the basic shade must be estimated and mixed in afterwards. Thus, 2 oz of 50 per cent grey hair would require 1 oz of the basic shade and 1 oz of white; 2 oz of 25 per cent grey would require $1\frac{1}{2}$ oz of basic shade and $\frac{1}{2}$ oz of white. The basic shade may be any colour, from blonde to black.

When adding white hair it is advisable to use a small quantity at first as it is easier to add more than to take some out, and only an experienced posticheur can make a correct estimate of the amount of white needed to match a given pattern.

3 WEAVING

An indispensable part of boardwork is the skill of weaving. It is a craft that cannot be replaced by any machine process. Neat and careful weaving is an essential attribute of a good boardworker. For the process of weaving, three threads of silk are usually used, technically referred to as strings. It is important to weave the root ends of the hair around the strings, and to keep these short and level.

The weaving sticks (see page 5) fit into wooden clamps or screws and these fix on to the work-bench about 18 in. apart [*Figure* 2]. To prepare the sticks for use, wind weaving silk on to each of the three grooves on the right-hand stick. Place a small wedge of paper underneath the silk on each groove. First attach the end of the silk to the paper and then wind the silk round the paper and the groove together, smoothly and evenly. This is done so that each silk can be tightened or loosened individually. It is important that all the silks are of equal tension when weaving. To fix up ready for use, put the left-hand stick in the clamp. This has a nail which should be level with the centre groove on the right-hand stick. Unwind the silks and tie them together in a single knot, then make a slip-knot which runs against this single knot. The silks can then easily be hooked or un-hooked on the nail [see *Figure* 2]. Adjust the tension so that all three strings are even and moderately tight and the weaving frame is ready to commence weaving. A jockey will be required to hold the weft from coming undone. There are five main kinds of weaving:

1 Once-in weaving.
2 Twice-in weaving.
3 Thrice-in weaving.
4 Three-string fly-weft.
5 Two-string fly-weft.

ONCE-IN WEAVING

Sometimes called flat-weft, this is the most commonly used type of weaving and comprises the main bulk of the weaving for most types of postiche made of weft.

Method: For the purpose of this and all other types of weaving, imagine that the strings are numbered 1, 2, and 3 starting at the lowest thread [*Figure* 9(1)].

Set up the weaving frame and place the hair in the drawing brushes with the root end protruding 2 in. Draw out a fine section of hair and hold it in the left hand 2 in. from the root end, push it forward from back to front between strings 1 and 2; take it over the top and bring it forward again between 3 and 2; move it down and under the bottom string and bring forward between 2 and 3; take it over the top again and forward between 3 and 2. Finally, push the roots back between 2 and 1. Now slide the hair from right to left until the roots are short, not more than $\frac{3}{4}$ in. Tighten the hair on the strings and push it along to the left. Put a jockey on the strings to prevent the weft from coming undone while the next one is being woven. *Figure* 9(1) shows exactly how the hair intertwines around the strings. Pull the hair out cleanly from the brushes. After a little practice it is easy to take hold of just the right amount of hair each time and this will ensure that the remaining hair stays neat in the brushes and the ends drawn out are level.

STARTING AND FINISHING KNOTS

These are the same for once-in, twice-in, thrice-in and three-string fly-weft.

When weaving the first piece of hair *only*, bring the long end of hair forward, and push it back between strings 1 and and 2 after tightening the hair on the strings, to form a starting-knot [*Figure* 9(4)]. When the next piece of hair is woven and pushed up against it, this will prevent the weaving from coming undone.

Continue taking fine pieces of hair and working neatly and evenly until the required amount of weaving is done. Then finish by doing the last weft as follows: instead of finally pushing back the roots between 2 and 1 in the usual place, bring them forward in front of the whole weft; separate

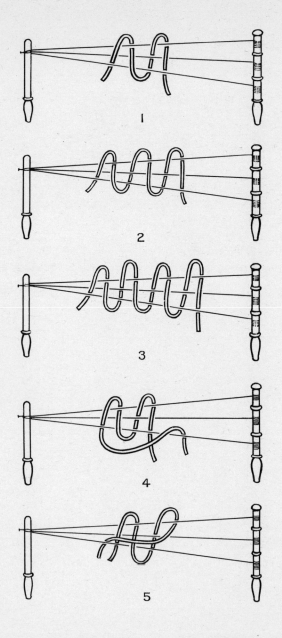

Figure 9. (1) 'Once-in' weaving; (2) 'Twice-in' weaving; (3) 'Thrice-in' weaving; (4) Starting knot; (5) Finishing knot.

strings 1 and 2 and push the hair roots in between them to make a finishing-knot as shown in *Figure* 9(5).

TWICE-IN WEAVING

This is very similar to once-in weaving, except that the hair is given an extra turn round the silks, which results in a more widely-spaced weft. It could be used if a longer length of weaving was required without using extra hair.

Method: Put in a starting-knot as previously described and then push the root end of hair from back to front, forward between strings 1 and 2; take over 2 and 3 and bring forward between 3 and 2, in front of 2 and 1, under and behind 1 and 2, forward between 2 and 3, over 3 and forward between 3 and 2, in front of 2 and 1, under 1 and behind 1 and 2, forward between 2 and 3, over 3 and forward between 3 and 2 and finally back between 2 and 1 [*Figure* 9(2)]. When sufficient weaving is done, end off with a finishing-knot.

THRICE-IN WEAVING

Also called crop or wig-weft, it is used for making complete wigs of weft where a widely spaced weft is needed, because it may take from 25 to 30 yards of weaving for a complete wig. As its name implies, the hair is taken yet once again round the silks before finishing [*Figure* 9(3)].

FLY-WEFT
THREE-STRING FLY-WEFT

Also called top-row, is very fine weaving using only four to six hairs at a time. It is done in a similar manner to once-in weaving except that the roots are not finally pushed back between strings 2 and 1 [*Figure* 10(4)].

TWO-STRING FLY-WEFT

Like three-string fly-weft it is also called top-row. Either kind of fly-weft is used for the top row of postiche wherever an extra neat finish is required. Their choice is largely a matter of

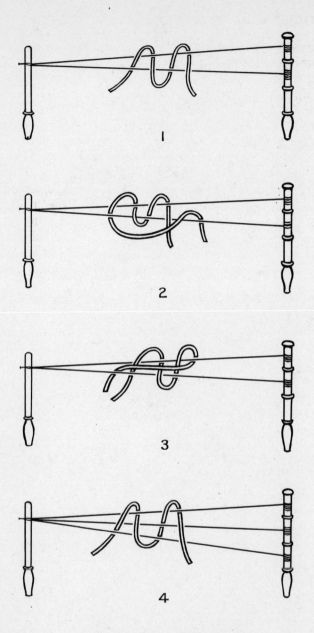

Figure 10. (1) Two-string fly-weft; (2)
Starting knot; (3) Finishing knot;
(4) Three-string fly-weft.

preference as either kind can look equally neat if the weaving is done very finely. The starting and finishing knots for two-string fly-weft are shown in *Figures* 10(2) and 10(3). Before starting to weave, slacken off the bottom string, ready to work on the top two strings only. Intertwine the hair as shown in *Figure* 10(1). This weaving is very simple, and easy to follow from the diagram.

All weaving should be pressed on completion with heated pressing or pinching irons. It is advisable to do this while the work is still on the strings. Heat the irons, put a piece of tissue paper over the weaving and pinch the weft between the two flat metal discs of the irons. Move the irons and paper along the weft until the whole length has been pressed.

4 USES OF HAIR WEFT

When hair has been woven it is known as hair weft and may be further designated: flat-weft, wig-weft, or: once-in weaving, twice-in weaving, thrice-in weaving, according to the way in which it has been woven. Each piece of postiche described in this chapter is made of hair weft of one or more kinds, and varying amounts of weft are needed for each one. Hair weft may be made into finished postiche by the following methods:

1 It may be wound round and round a centre stem as in the case of switches and pin-curls;
2 It may be folded in various ways and the layers of weft stitched together e.g. in marteaux and diamond mesh;
3 It can be stitched onto some type of foundation made of net or galloon, e.g. a weft wig which is a complete wig made of hair weft stitched onto a suitable foundation.

SWITCHES
A THREE-STEM SWITCH

Switches may be made of a single stem, or of two or three stems, thus enabling the hair to be coiled or plaited. When making a three-stem switch, the hair is drawn off, and most of the very short hair is taken out. From the remainder, the longest hair is taken out to use for the top-row, enough to do 2 in. of weaving. The rest of the hair is divided into three equal portions – one portion to be used for each stem.

Weaving

Set up the weaving sticks leaving at least 6 in. of clear silk before starting to weave. Using the longest hair, weave 2 in.

of two-string fly-weft for the top-row; keep it very fine and neat and begin with a starting-knot. Divide the remaining quantity of hair into three equal portions, one for each stem. Take one portion, and continue weaving in moderately fine once-in weaving until all this section of hair has been used. Do not leave a space between the fly-weft and the once-in weaving. Gradually bring the weaving finer towards the end, and end off with a finishing-knot. You have now completed weaving the top-row and one stem.

Twist the weft around the left-hand weaving peg and commence the second stem, leaving at least 8 in. clear on the silks. Take another section of hair, commence with a starting-knot and weave all the hair in once-in weaving, finishing off as before with a finishing-knot.

Again leave 8 in. of clear silk and weave the third stem in the same way. Unwind the weaving and carefully press all the work with hot pinching irons. The work is then ready for cutting down and winding into stems. Cut off $1\frac{1}{2}$ in. from the end of each stem and tie in a knot. Do not tie a knot at the beginning of each stem, only at the end.

Winding

Fix the twisting machine to the bench, with tail cord ready wound, and commence by sewing the end of the weaving $\frac{1}{4}$ in. from the end of the tail cord [*Figure* 11(1)]. Hold the weft in the left hand and with the right hand turn the cord, winding the weft closely and tightly and advancing up the tail cord at each turn, just the width of the weft [*Figure* 11(2)]. Turn the knob on the twisting machine to the left every now and then and it will tighten the cord and help the winding process. Put a stitch through the weft and the cord at intervals if a long length of weft is to be wound. You will find that the hair will run slightly along the silks as it is wound and this is the reason for leaving extra silk between the stems. When all the weft is wound up, sew the end securely, fasten off the sewing silk, and and cut the tail cord leaving about $\frac{1}{2}$ in. of cord.

Wind the second stem in exactly the same way and cut off the cord. Finally, wind the last stem, which is the one with the top-row attached. Wind in the same way, up to where the top-row commences, and then stitch through the weft and tail cord securely but do not cut the tail cord. Take the other two stems and sew to the first one as neatly as possible and wind a $\frac{1}{4}$ in. of the top-row round them, leaving the remaining top-row to be wound later. Now cover a length of tail cord, about $\frac{3}{4}$ in. with sewing silk to match the hair [*Figure* 11(3)], by running silk round the tail cord. Cut off the tail cord and double this back to form a loop and stitch firmly [*Figure* 11(4)]. Tie the loop up to the twisting machine and wind the top row round it. This should be done very neatly, stitching right through the cord and weft with almost invisible stitches. The top may be finished off by running silk round and round, thus hiding all the actual weaving. Put a piece of tissue paper round the loop and press carefully with hot pinching irons [*Figure* 11(5)].

A switch made like this should be of good shape and nicely tapered. It can be plaited and worn as a chignon [*Figure* 11(6)]. The hair must be prepared and used according to the lengths available and the finished results required. Always use tail cord and sewing silk to match the hair colour, and work as neatly and firmly as possible.

A TWO-STEM SWITCH

The procedure is similar to the making of a three-stem switch except that after weaving the top-row, the hair is divided into two equal parts instead of three and two lengths of weaving are done, one for each stem.

The finish for the loop is exactly the same as described for a three-stem switch. The two stems are stitched together before covering the tail cord for the loop and before winding the top-row. A two-stem switch can be coiled but not plaited.

A ONE-STEM SWITCH

This is made by weaving a top-row and one stem. Set up the twisting machine. Stitch the end of the weaving to the end of the tail cord [*Figure* 11(1)], wind tightly and evenly, advancing up the cord just the width of the weft at each turn [*Figure* 11(2)]. Wind to the beginning of the top-row. Cover a length of tail cord with silk to match the hair colour by running it round and round the tail cord [*Figure* 11(3)]. Cut off the tail cord and stitch it over into a loop [*Figure* 11(4)]. Finish by running the sewing silk round to hide the top-row of weaving. Take one stitch through the loop and three or four invisible stitches to fasten off [*Figure* 11(5)].

The uses of a one-stem switch are limited as it cannot be coiled or plaited and it may appear thin unless made of curled hair.

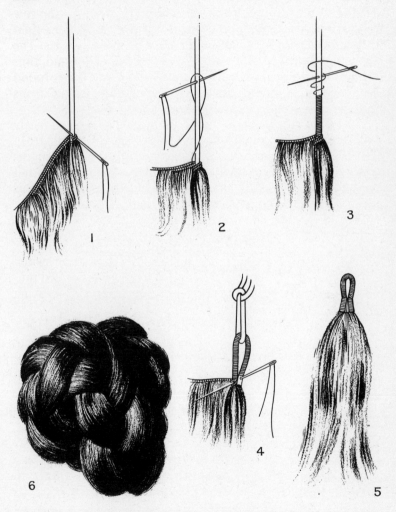

Figure 11. Winding a one-stem switch

MARTEAUX

Marteaux are made of hair weft stitched up flat instead of being wound up on a central stem like a switch, and may be of any required width. Two or more can be stitched together to form into a chignon. A single large marteau, mounted on a postiche comb or postiche clip, may be made into ringlet bunches. *Figure* 12(4) shows a waved marteau attached to a postiche clip. *Figure* 32 shows the method of covering a postiche comb to enable it to be sewn to the top of the marteau.

Method: A top-row is woven first allowing twice the width of the finished marteau plus $\frac{1}{4}$ in.: thus a 1 in. marteau would require $2\frac{1}{4}$ in. of top-row and a 4 in. marteau would need $8\frac{1}{4}$ in. of top-row. Use the longest hair for the top-row and weave this first, then continue in fine once-in weaving.

Weaving

To make a 2 in. marteau set up the weaving sticks and place the hair in the brushes. Weave $4\frac{1}{4}$ in. of fine top-row in two-string fly-weft and continue without leaving a space using the remainder of the hair in moderately fine once-in weaving. Measure the weaving before putting a finishing-knot and make sure there is the right amount to make an exact number of folds plus $\frac{1}{2}$ in. for turnings. Thus, again for a 2 in. marteau, either $4\frac{1}{2}$ in. or $6\frac{1}{2}$ in. or more of once-in weaving could be used. Press well, cut down $1\frac{1}{2}$ in. from the end of the weaving and tie the silks in a knot close down to the end of the weaving.

Sewing-up

Turn over the first fold slightly less than 2 in. in width, with the second fold slightly in advance of the previous one. Commence to sew at the end where the weaving finished and sew from the centre of the lower fold to the centre of the one above, right through the actual weft [*Figure* 12(1)].

Be sure to stitch securely at the end of each fold and then turn over the third fold, again slightly in advance of the previous one and stitch as before. Continue sewing up the folds maintaining the correct width of 2 in. until the first half of the top row has been sewn [*Figure* 12(2)]. Stitch the final fold completely level and take the stitches either through and through or over and over.

A 2 in. marteau may be finished off with two small loops, one at each end, made by buttonholing over six strands of thread. Press well with pinching irons and wave or curl as required [*Figure* 12(3)].

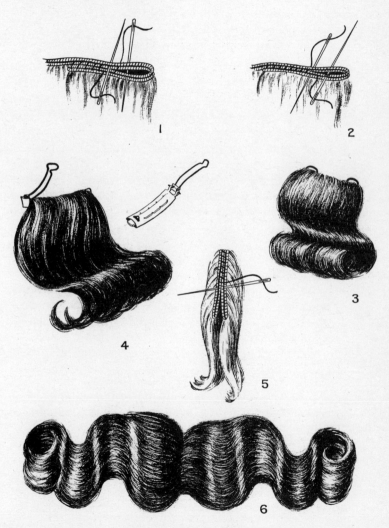

Figure 12. Sewing a marteau and swathe

D

SWATHES

A swathe can most easily be made by making two 2 in. marteaux of 6 in. to 8 in. waved hair. Stitch the two marteaux together through and through the top rows [*Figure* 12(5)]. This will make all the stitching invisible and give a certain amount of lift in the centre of the swathe. It can then be set to appear as a continuous wave with curled ends and is useful for hiding the back of short hair or growing ends [*Figure* 12(6)].

Two 4 to 5 in. marteaux stitched together in this way can easily be dressed to give the appearance of a french pleat at the back of the head. The ends are combed in at the sides with the client's own hair.

PIN-CURLS

Pin-curls are quite small curls which can be added wherever an extra curl is required. The smaller curls may be used for forehead curls or fringes; the larger curls dressed in puffs or waves can be added to the coiffure in any place where they may be required. They can be made in a lighter colour than the main shade and worn to give the appearance of blonde streaks in the hair. There are three ways of making pin-curls:

1 An ordinary pin-curl which is wound up on a pin, usually quite a small curl.
2 A pin-wave which is about the same size, but the weft is stitched up flat and finished with a loop.
3 A pin-curl marteau which is a larger curl, stitched flat at first and finished with a pin.

1 To make an ordinary pin-curl

Set up the weaving sticks; place the hair in the brushes and weave a top-row of fine two-string fly-weft usually $\frac{3}{4}$ in. Weave the remaining hair in fine once-in weaving, usually 3 in. to 4 in. Press with pinching irons and cut down. Attach the end of the weaving to the end of the pin-wire by turning up the extreme ends of wire into a loop [*Figure* 13(*A*1)]. Wind the hair weft round and round as tightly as possible and finish off securely [*Figure* 13(*A*2)]. Neaten the top by running sewing silk round to hide the top row of weaving. The wire takes the place of the tail cord to form the stem [*Figure* 13(*A*3)].

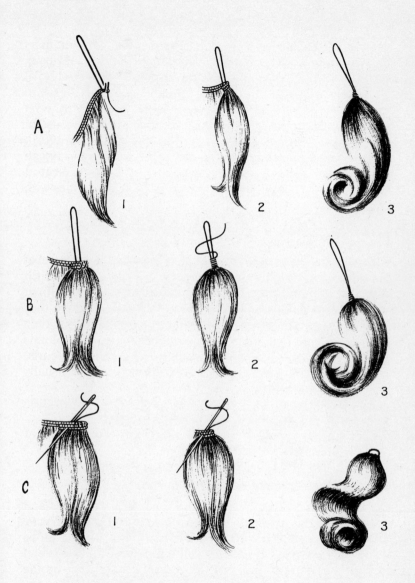

Figure 13. Making a pin-curl (*A*); pin-curl marteau (*B*); and pin-wave (*C*).

2 To make a pin-wave

This requires the same amount of weaving as an ordinary pin-curl. Fold over the end of the weaving ½ in. and stitch the two folds together advancing the second row slightly higher than the first [*Figure* 13(*C*1)]. Continue sewing up the weft in folds, round and round, advancing with each fold and tapering in, until the top row is reached. The mount should taper from ½ in. to ¼ in. in width [*Figure* 13(*C*2)]. Sew the top row round keeping the final two rows level and sewing either through and through, or over and over. Finish off with a small loop by buttonholing over six strands of silk [*Figure* 13(*C*3)].

3 A pin-curl marteau

This contains more hair than the two previous curls. Weave ¾ in. of top-row and follow on with 4 in. to 8 in. of fine once-in weaving, putting starting- and finishing-knots. Press the weaving and cut down.

To stitch up commence by folding over the end of the weft ¾ in. to 1 in. and stitching flat, gradually tapering the folds until four or more have been stitched up [*Figure* 13(*B*1)]. Take a pin-curl wire, turn up the ends, and stitch in firmly. Continue sewing up, and tapering in, each fold [*Figure* 13(*B*2)]. Finish by winding the top-row as described for the first type of pin-curl [*Figure* 13(*B*3)]. Dress out in curls or waves as required.

A DOUBLE-LOOP CLUSTER

A double-loop cluster is a stem of short curly hair with a loop at each end. It can be worn as a chignon in the nape to hide short hair, as a cluster of curls on the crown, or across the forehead as a curled fringe. The two loops help to attach the postiche firmly to the hair by enabling pins to be placed through them.

Weaving

Set up the weaving sticks and weave 1½ in. of fine top-row on two strings commencing with a starting-knot; continue straight on in fine once-in weaving for about 18 in. (more or

Figure 14. Winding a double-loop cluster

less according to the size required), then weave another 1½ in.
of top-row and put a finishing-knot. Heat the pressing irons.
Press all the weaving, and cut down leaving at least 8 in. of
silk at the end. Do not tie knots at either end of the weaving.

Winding and finishing

Fix the twisting machine to the work bench. Measure the
exact centre of the weaving. Pull out a length of tail cord on
the twisting machine and sew the centre of the weaving 10 in.
from the end of the tail cord [*Figure* 14(1)]. Leave this end,
and half the weaving. Wind up one half of the weaving in
exactly the same way as a one-stem switch. When the top-row
is reached cover the cord and make a loop [*Figure* 14(2)],
finishing off with the top-row.

Now tie up the loose end of tail cord that was left at the
beginning [*Figure* 14(3)], and wind up the other half of the
weaving to the top-row. Finish off in the same way by making
a loop and winding the second top-row. This makes a continuous 4 in. to 6 in. stem of curled hair with a loop at each
end [*Figure* 14(4)].

Press the loops, pin through them onto a malleable block,
and set the hair into small curls which can be dressed as
required. *Figure* 14(5) shows a double-loop cluster of curls.

5 VARIATIONS OF HAIR WEFT

DIAMOND OR HONEYCOMB MESH

This is a method of stitching up hair weft in varying shapes to make an extremely light adaptable piece of postiche. A unique feature is that of replacing one string on the weaving sticks with fine wire; this gives strength to the weft and enables it to be stitched up into an open mesh foundation which, while retaining its shape, can be bent to the shape of the head in the position in which it is to be worn. The different shapes of foundation have different names, e.g.:

1 Diamond-mesh marteau
2 Diamond-mesh cluster
3 *Cache peigne*

The first two are self explanatory. The *cache peigne* is stitched up into a diamond-shaped foundation and the lengths of hair arranged so that short curled hair can be dressed into curls just below the crown of the head with ringlets of longer hair hanging down below the nape. It is attached to the head by means of a postiche comb from which its name is derived. *Cache peigne* means literally, a hidden comb.

Method: To make a diamond-mesh cluster with a finished foundation 5 in. $\times$ $1\frac{1}{2}$ in. Replace the central string on the weaving stick with fine wire. Put in a starting-knot, weave 26 in. of fine once-in weaving and put in a finishing-knot. Heat the pinching irons and press all the weaving before cutting down. Tie each end of the silk in a knot and turn in the ends of the wire so that the weaving cannot slip along and come loose.

Measure the weaving carefully and fold it over in four equal folds each $6\frac{1}{2}$ in. long, folded backwards and forwards, not round and round. Each fold will be longer than the size re-

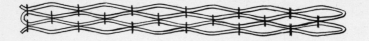

Figure 15. Sewing of diamond mesh: (1) weaving folded in four
equal lengths; (2) diamond-shaped mesh; (3) finished
diamond-mesh cluster of curls.

quired for the finished mount but this will be taken up in the sewing. Take the first two folds and stitch together at equal intervals every $\frac{3}{4}$ in. Then sew the third fold to the second fold, also at $\frac{3}{4}$ in. intervals but arrange the stitches to fall at intervals exactly between the first row of stitches [*Figure* 15(1)]. Take up another row, again arranging the stitches exactly in the centre of the previous ones.

Fasten the ends securely and pull out the weaving into diamond-shaped meshes. Press the stitched points with the tip of a marcel waving iron which will fit in between the rows of stitching. Pull the rows of stitching slightly apart to give them the required width and the typical diamond-shaped mesh will be apparent [*Figure* 15(2)].

A small loop should be made at each end of the foundation by buttonholing over six strands of silk. This is to enable the diamond mesh to be pinned to the hair. Set the hair in curls and dress out. *Figure* 15(3) shows a finished diamond mesh cluster of curls.

TORSADES MADE OF WEFT

Torsades can be made in various ways: by making a two-stem switch and stitching short curled hair at one end; by coiling together two one-stem switches; or by using four marteaux sewn together in pairs, one marteau being taken from each side, over to the opposite side.

The simplest form of torsade is made to appear as a continuous coil of hair with curls at each end [*Figure* 16(3)]. This can most easily be made by weaving two stems of 12 in. to 14 in. curled hair in fine once-in weaving. The hair should not be very tapered. Wind each stem and cut off, leaving about 1 in. of tail cord. Stitch these two stems together but do not make a loop as you would for a switch.

Weave 3 in. to 4 in. of fine three-string fly-weft using short curled hair of the same colour as the main part. Press the roots down and stitch this weft neatly round and round the 1 in. of tail cord but facing the opposite way to the main bulk of hair. Arrange it just to overlap the weaving at the top of the two stems [*Figure* 16(2)]. The stems are then back-combed and coiled together to within 3 to 4 in. from the end. Tie with a strand of hair and curl both ends of the torsade to match.

1

2

3

Figure 16. Torsades

There are other ways of making torsades, with curls in the centre as well as at each end, but these are more complicated and usually have a small net foundation in the centre.

Yet another way is to make two one-stem switches and coil them together so that 3 to 4 in. of hair extends beyond the loop at each end [*Figure* 16(1)]. Tie with a strand of hair by the loop and curl the ends as before.

WEFT WIGS

It is possible to make complete wigs of hair weft but these are rarely made nowadays as it is difficult to avoid an obviously 'wiggy' appearance. Modern stage and film work demand a much higher standard of hairwork. Owing to the good lighting now available, any defects of make-up or coiffure are shown up more clearly than hitherto.

The foundation is similar in shape to that made for a wig for normal wear, and the method of making the foundation is described in the second part of this book (pages 60 to 73). The main part of the wig is made of wig weft and this is sewn in rows to the foundation. The outer edge is done first and this is done with the fine fly-weft. Each row of weft is sewn on about $\frac{1}{4}$ in. apart and a complete wig will need from 25 to 30 yards of weft. If a parting is to be included, this is marked out on the foundation and the main part of the wig made first. This type of wig can be made more cheaply than a knotted wig because, although many yards of weaving are required, it does not take as much time to make as a knotted wig.

A recent innovation is a machine-made wig which is made by machine-stitching rows of hair onto a net foundation which is simply shaped like a skull cap with an elastic running round the outer edge. This is reasonably satisfactory provided that the wig is dressed with the hair falling towards the face, so hiding the edge of the wig. A bouffant style, where considerable back-combing is used, is also of help in hiding the foundation.

CRÊPE HAIR

The making of crêpe hair is comparatively simple. For this,

it is customary to use hair of 6 in. to 8 in. in length. Prepare the right-hand weaving stick with two strings of strong carpet thread instead of the usual weaving silk.

Place the weaving sticks in the wooden clamps. Tie a knot to hold the two strings together and a slip knot to attach them to the nail on the left-hand stick. *Figure* 17 shows this and also illustrates the process of weaving crêpe hair.

Keep the threads taut while weaving and the strings of equal tension. Place the hair in the drawing brushes with the root-end projecting and draw off a fairly thick piece of hair. Hold it firmly with the left hand and start to weave by placing the root end close up to the knot and intertwining the free end in and out as shown in *Figure* 17(1): that is, forward between strings 1 and 2, over and behind 2, forward between 2 and 1, under and behind 1, forward again between 1 and 2.

When the first two movements are completed take hold of both ends of the hair and intertwine them together round the strings. Continue until the whole length of hair is used up. It is important to tighten the hair on the strings and to push it up to the left at each turn. It will help to distribute the hair evenly on the strings if it is given a slight twist each time that it is taken through the strings [*Figure* 17(2)].

When the first piece of hair is woven, put a jockey on the strings to prevent it from coming undone, draw another piece of hair of similar thickness and weave it in exactly the same way.

Continue until all the hair is used up, winding the weft round the left-hand peg and releasing more string from the right as the work proceeds. When finished, cut the threads and tie a knot on the end close down to the weaving to prevent it from coming undone.

Place the weft in a pan and cover with water. Boil for 30 minutes or more, lift out, and allow to drain. Afterwards place in the postiche oven to bake for several hours until thoroughly dry. The weft is stored on the strings until required for use.

Crêpe hair is useful for adding bulk by mixing with straighter hair for switches, wigs, or other hairwork. It is the most satisfactory medium for making beards and moustaches for

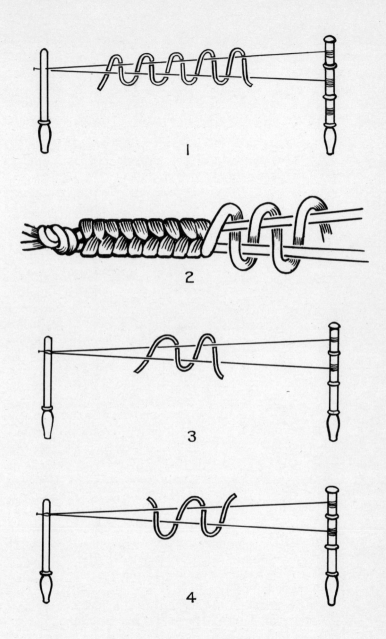

Figure 17. Weaving crêpe-hair (1 and 2); and crêpe pads (3 and 4).

theatrical use, particularly when these are built up directly onto the face. It is employed in the making of pads or frizzettes, pompadour rolls and is also used for covering chignon frames.

CRÊPE PADS

To make a crêpe pad, the weaving sticks are set up in the same way as for the making of crêpe hair. Use carpet thread to match the colour of the hair being used. Free a quantity of crêpe hair from the strings and hackle it out. It then becomes full and fluffy in appearance. Place the fluffy crêpe hair in the drawing brushes or leave it in the hackle and put one brush on top of the hackle.

Each pad has a fine loop and this is woven first by drawing out a fine piece of hair and weaving it exactly as directed for making crêpe hair but very much finer. About ¾ in. to 1 in. of fine weft will be required.

The following wefts are drawn thicker and each weft is *woven in the middle of the piece of hair*. This is not done for any other form of weaving. Thus both ends of the hair are free and of equal length.

The first weft is woven in the same way as two-string flyweft; that is, forming the letter M on the strings [*Figure* 17(3)]. The second weft is inserted in the opposite way forming a W on the strings. These two wefts are clearly illustrated in *Figure* 17(3 and 4). The work is continued, alternating each weft so that the hair stands away equally all round the strings.

The actual length of weft required will be less than the length of the finished pad; for example, a 6 in. pad requires about 4½ in. of weaving. The hair will hold more firmly if the last two wefts are done much finer, the final one being woven in the form of a finishing-knot made in the same way as shown for two-string fly-weft [*Figure* 10(4)]. The ends of the string are now cut and tied down to the weaving in a knot which should be cut off neatly.

While the weaving is still secured to the hook on the left-hand weaving stick, comb all the hair down and roll it between the hands to make a well-shaped pad. When a satisfactory shape has been obtained, trim off the extreme ends of the hair crêpe. The loop end is then finished off by folding over the fine weaving into a loop as neatly as possible.

Roll the pad in tissue paper and bake in a warm oven to help it to retain its shape. Pads may be used singly or in twos or threes.

POMPADOUR ROLLS

A roll is made in very much the same way as a pad but as a loop is required at each end, it is finished off differently. Commence by weaving a fine section for the loop and continue as described for pads. A roll is usually 8 in. or 10 in. when finished.

Weave $1\frac{1}{2}$ in. less than the length required for the finished roll. Put in two fine wefts and then a finishing-knot. Do not cut off the strings yet. Comb all the hair towards the right, rolling it into shape with the hands. Gather together the extreme ends of the hair and weave a fine section of crêpe weft the same as the one done at the beginning. Now cut it down and sew the loops at each end neatly into position, hiding the ends of thread by running a fine strand of hair round and round. Roll into shape and bake in the oven to give firmness.

A pompadour roll as its name implies is used to give height to a pompadour dressing and is pinned into position behind the hair line, the woman's own hair being then dressed over it.

PART II

Foundational
Postiche

6 PREPARING THE PATTERN

The term foundational postiche refers to all types of postiche made on a net foundation, as distinct from postiche made of hair weft (described in Part I). The net is made into a foundation shape and afterwards implanted with hair by means of knotting. Each piece of postiche is made for a particular individual. A pattern is cut and fitted, because a wig is as much an individual possession as a dress, or a pair of spectacles. There are many different foundation shapes, each of which serves a distinct purpose.

A wig has a foundation which covers the entire area of the scalp and can form a complete dressing by itself. It may be used in cases of severe loss of hair and, for this purpose alone, over 10,000 wigs are supplied annually by the National Health Service. These are supplied to the wearer at a fraction of the original cost. Many other wigs are made purely for adornment; these may vary in cost tremendously depending on the quality, colour, and texture of the hair used, the type of foundation material, and the method of producing the parting, if one is included.

Smaller pieces of postiche are made for various purposes; usually, to hide loss of hair on part of the scalp; or as an addition in the form of a chignon to elaborate a style. These must of course be made in the same colour hair as the wearer's natural hair shade.

A complete wig may be any colour and is, in fact, often worn purely to create a change of colour without having to dye or bleach the wearer's own hair.

MEASURING

Before any foundation can be made it is necessary to take accurate measurements. These, as a general guide, are taken as follows:

The circumference

This is taken round the head from about ½ in. above the hairline in the nape of the neck, above one ear, across the front ½ in. above the hairline, above the other ear and down to the starting point in the nape. In an adult it may vary from 19 in. to 24 in. but 21 in. to 22 in. are the most usual measurements. This is shown on the chart, see *Figure* 18(1).

Forehead to nape

Place the tape-measure exactly on the hairline at the centre front, take it over the crown and down to the hairline in the nape of the neck [*Figure* 18(2)].

Ear-to-ear across the front

This measurement is just in front of one ear across the forehead right on the hairline to a similar position in front of the opposite ear [*Figure* 18(3)].

Ear-to-ear over the crown

Now measure from just above one ear, over the crown to just above the other ear [*Figure* 18(4)].

Temple-peak to temple-peak, round the back

When taking this measurement take care that the tape-measure is kept level round the back of the head [*Figure* 18(5)].

Nape of neck

One final measurement is taken and this is across the nape of the neck [*Figure* 18(6)].

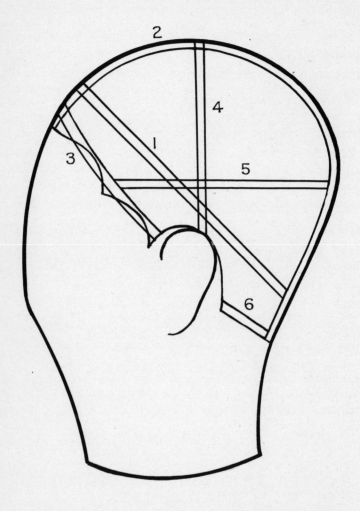

Figure 18. Method of measuring wigs: (1) circumference; (2) forehead to nape; (3) ear-to-ear across the front; (4) ear-to-ear over the crown; (5) temple-peak to temple-peak round the back; (6) nape of neck.

Other details required by the wigmaker

If a parting is to be included, give the length and the distance from the centre. If no parting is required this must be stated.

Abnormalities

Make a note and give the position of any abnormality of the scalp, such as bumps or cysts; or of an unusually shaped head.

Details of hair

This must include lengths at various places; the exact colour and quality; and whether straight, waved or curly hair is to be used. A pattern of hair should be enclosed.

Style

Make a detailed note of the style to be dressed. Possibly, a photograph or sketch could be enclosed.

RECORDS

It is advisable to keep a record of all completed work. This is most conveniently done on a card index, or printed on an envelope so that a hair pattern and perhaps a photograph can be enclosed. An example of a typical chart showing the requirements of a wigmaker, and providing information for the hairdresser's index appears on page 56.

CUTTING THE PATTERN FOR WIGS, TRANSFORMATIONS, AND SEMI-TRANSFORMATIONS

An experienced wigmaker can, and usually does, make the mount of a wig without cutting a pattern. He may draw it on the block first or point it out right away with $\frac{1}{4}$ centimetre galloon.

RECORD CARD   No.......

Hair pattern enclosed

Name

Address

Type of postiche, e.g. wig, transformation, etc..........................
Measurements required: *Inches*
    1 Circumference ....
    2 Forehead to nape ....
    3 Ear-to-ear over forehead ....
    4 Ear-to-ear over the top...................................
    5 Temple-to-temple
      round the back ....
    6 Nape of neck ....
Parting details:
Length ....
Position ....
Hair details:
Colour ....
Length ....
Curled or straight ....
Style ....

Any abnormality ....
Price quoted ....
Date required ....

....
....
....

There are advantages however in working to a pattern. It can be cut and tried on the client before mounting, thus ensuring a correct fit. It can also be made of light or coloured paper contrasting to the net which will make the knotting easier to see.

The outer part of a wig to a depth of two or more inches in front and one inch in the nape is made of fine net and a pattern may be cut for this part. The crown is filled in with coarser net and no pattern is required for this as it simply requires filling in after the mount is made.

The depth of the mount, in front, is determined by the position and length of the parting. If no parting is included, a reasonable depth is 2 in. at the centre front.

Figure 19 shows a basic shape for a wig or transformation pattern assuming the measurements to be: circumference $21\frac{1}{2}$ in., ear-to-ear across the front 11 in., no parting, and nape of neck 4 in.

The pattern is cut and mounted on a block $\frac{1}{2}$ in. larger than the actual circumference of the head. This $\frac{1}{2}$ in. is taken up afterwards with the tension springs (see page 72). The patterns for a wig and a transformation are identical, although there is a slight difference in mounting them because a transformation has an opening at the centre back.

To cut the pattern according to the measurements given, take a strip of paper 22 in. long and 2 in. deep and fold it in half lengthways. The fold represents the centre front so that the pattern will be cut symmetrically. Measure $5\frac{1}{2}$ in. from this fold and mark it with a dot. This represents the ear-peak. Now, draw in the front edge and shape it in the way the hair grows working from the centre-front hairline. It should be similar to *Figure* 19(1). Then start to work from the upper edge at the centre-back of the pattern: measure 1 in. down and mark it with a dot; measure $2\frac{1}{4}$ in. along the top edge and mark that. From this mark measure down $1\frac{1}{2}$ in. and use a dot to mark this measurement. Rule a line from this dot to the one at the centre back. The pattern now looks like *Figure* 19(2). Finally draw in the edge of the mount, shaping it to fit over the ear as shown in *Figure* 19(3).

Cut out the front edge of the mount, keeping the two halves of the paper level and the pattern is ready to put on the block.

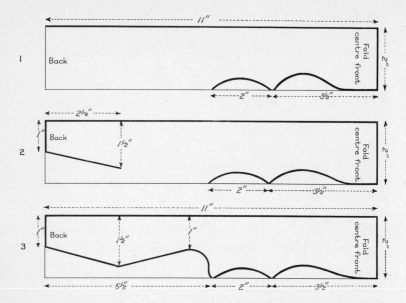

Figure 19. Cutting instructions for wig and transformation patterns

It is noticeable that the neck-measurement given was 4 in. but that on each half of the mount $2\frac{1}{4}$ in. have been allowed. This is because the wig is made on a block $\frac{1}{2}$ in. larger than the actual circumference of the head and the extra amount is allowed for in the nape, where it will be taken up with the tension springs.

If a parting is to be included and it has to be longer than 2 in., the mount is extended $\frac{1}{2}$ in. beyond the length of the parting, and shaped to the remainder of the mount as seen in *Figure* 20(1) and (2) which show left-hand and right-hand partings of different lengths. Sometimes a mount may be deeper at the centre front for a pompadour dressing and in this case it would be extended at the centre front.

SEMI-TRANSFORMATIONS

To cut a pattern for a semi-transformation the following measurements are required:

  1 Ear-to-ear across the front hairline.
  2 Actual length of mount required.

3 Depth of mount at centre front.

4 Details of parting, if one is to be included.

A semi-transformation is usually worn by a person suffering from loss of hair at the frontal position only and the mount covers this portion of the head. It usually ends just above or behind the ears. The hair is dressed to fall in with the wearer's own hair.

A careful study of the comparative sketches in *Figure* 20 will show clearly how to cut the pattern. It is similar to a wig or transformation pattern except that it tapers off to a point just above or behind the ears. It is held in position on the head by the galloon bind, which is left long enough to encircle the head, and by inserting tension springs at each end. These fasten at the centre back with a hook and eye [see *Figure* 26 (2*c*)]. Alternatively if the wearer's hair is fairly short at the back and would not hide the galloon bind, it can have a piece of fine, round elastic instead.

Positional springs are placed at the salient points on the mount itself to hold the foundation down to the head [see *Figure* 26(1*b*)].

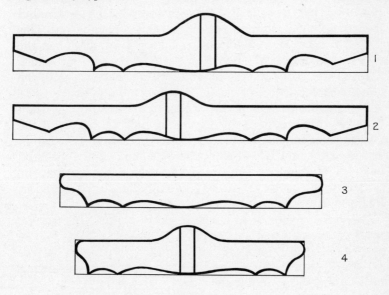

Figure 20. Patterns for wigs and transformations (1 and 2); and semi-transformations (3 and 4).

7 FOUNDATION MAKING

WIGS

The measurements used in cutting the pattern, do not include all those which were taken. The others are used for mounting the pattern on the block. Having chosen the most suitable block, take the pattern and point the centre front at the approximate position of the hairline. Turn the point outward, and put another point at the inner edge of the centre fold, turning this, too, out over the edge of the pattern.

Take the tape-measure, and measure the required distance from forehead to nape over the top of the block. Let us assume that it is 14 in. Take the pattern round the block and point it at the back in that position. Now, check the other measurements: ear-to-ear round the back and over the top, etc. It is fairly easy to adjust the pattern until it satisfies all the measurements. Use only just enough points to hold it in position.

The paper will have to be smoothed on to the block. If it is slightly moistened before it is put on, it will be easier to fit without too many creases.

The first piece of galloon to be put on is called 'the bind'. The galloon ribbon, which encircles the head, is the main aid to holding the wig in place. For this, use $\frac{1}{2}$ or $\frac{3}{4}$ centimetre galloon. Start at the centre back, put in a point and take the galloon round the head in the position in which the circumference was measured. The correct placing of this bind makes a considerable difference to the fit and balance of the finished postiche. A study of *Figure* 22(*a*) will show the exact position in which it should be placed.

Use as few points as possible to hold the bind in position for the time being. Take it right round to the centre back and cut off, but leave enough to join the ends together neatly.

Next, outline the outer edge of the mount with a $\frac{1}{4}$ or $\frac{1}{2}$ centimetre galloon [*Figure* 22(*b*)]. Again start at the centre back and place the block points, pointing outward, to hold it in position. Do not use more than are really necessary but more will be needed round the curved areas over the ears than on the straight lengths, and always use one at each main point: that is, at the ears, temple peaks, and the two slight peaks in the nape.

Take the galloon right round the outer edge until it meets again at the centre back, then cut off, leaving enough to make a neat join as before. Do the same round the inner edge of the mount but turn the points up towards the crown. The galloon should be in such a position that it is immediately inside the edge of the paper pattern and following it exactly. Join the ends of the bind together in a very neat run-and-fell seam. Do the same with the ends of the galloon outlining the inner and outer edges of the mount.

Cut a piece of foundation net 23 in. long and 3 in. wide. Point this down over the mount smoothing it round to have as few creases as possible, although some are inevitable. Point the centre front first and as the net is pointed down, remove any points in the galloon bind and replace them with points over the net, as they cannot be removed once the net is in position. Use as few points as possible to hold the net in place. There will be $\frac{1}{2}$ in. of net beyond the galloon both at the inner and outer edges at the centre front, and 1 in. at the centre back. The mount is now ready for sewing.

Sewing the foundation

Use sewing silk that matches the colour of the net and galloon. It is advisable to treat all sewing silk with beeswax before use. The best silk is usually used and it is bought in hanks. Untwist the hank carefully and rub beeswax over the silk, covering it adequately but not too thickly. Heat the pinching irons, put a piece of tissue paper round the hank of silk and run the pinching irons along the length of the hank, holding them over the tissue paper, until all trace of stickiness has disappeared. Cut the silk at each end of the hank and put in a folded piece of paper arranged as in *Figure* 21. The silk, cut in convenient lengths, will not twist and is now ready for use. The beeswax also strengthens it and preserves it from the action of perspiration from the scalp which can cause it to rot and break.

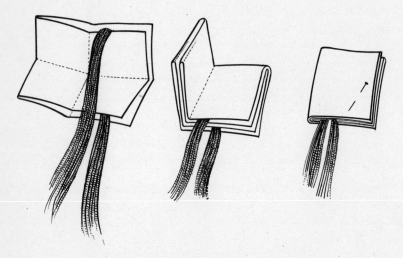

Figure 21. Sewing silk folded in paper and ready for use

Commence to sew the mount at the centre back and make a neat join at the ends of the net similar to a tiny run-and-fell seam. Use a finger shield for picking up the tip of the needle. Sew along each side of the bind, taking care not to move its position. Use a small, neat hemming stitch and remember that it is the underneath side of the work which will be visible on the finished mount.

Next sew all round the inner edge of the galloon which outlines the mount [see *Figure* 30(2.4)]. The net may need easing-in a little in places and this should be done without making a tuck in it.

Trim off the net leaving just over $\frac{1}{8}$ in. all round the mount [*Figure* 30(2.5)]: i.e., round both the crown section and the hairline. Remove any surplus block points as the work proceeds but enough must be left to hold the mount in place until it has been braced. This must be done all round the hairline edge for a wig mount and should be done at this stage.

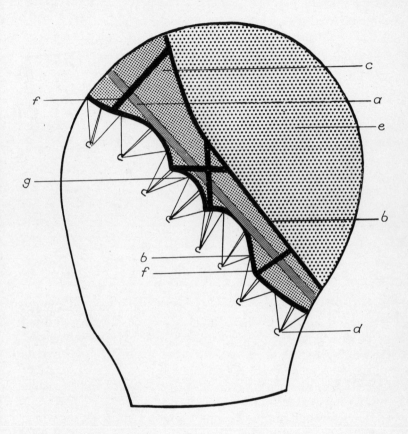

Figure 22. Completed wig mount: (*a*) the galloon bind; (*b*) galloon at hairline (or outer edge), and crown (or inner edge); (*c*) foundation net; (*d*) block points; (*e*) wig net; (*f*) positional springs; (*g*) bracing cotton.

Bracing

Place block points opposite each of the salient points 1 in. from the mount, and also about $1\frac{1}{2}$ in. apart all the way round the outer edge of the mount [*Figure* 22(*d*)]. Each point is hammered into the block at short distances, turned over with the pliers to form a loop and tapped into the block until both ends of the point are firmly in place, leaving a tiny loop through which a needle can be passed. It is important that these points are spaced correctly and put so that the bracing will hold down the peak points of the mount while it is being knotted. When all the block points are in place, turn back the edge of net, as the bracing is done to the galloon only.

Thread a length of strong white sewing-cotton and tie it to one of the points. The centre front is a convenient place at which to commence. Take a stitch up to the galloon immediately opposite to the point and back to the point passing the needle through the steel loop. Take another stitch through the galloon, to the right of the first one and half way to the next point. [See *Figure* 23.]

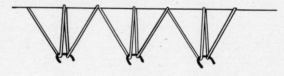

Figure 23. Bracing

Proceed to pass the needle through this point and then to the galloon and back to the point immediately opposite to it. A careful study of *Figures* 22, 25, and 26 will show exactly how the bracing is done.

This is one method of bracing but it should be pointed out that there are other ways of achieving the required result which is to hold the wig firmly on the block, particularly at the salient points, without having block points through the edge. If they were left in, it would be most difficult to do the subsequent knotting.

The outer edge of the mount can now be finished by turning in the $\frac{1}{8}$ in. of net and by blanket-stitching through the net and galloon all the way round the outer edge [see *Figure* 30(2.7)].

This stitching should be small and neat and should be

used to take in any slackness at the edge so that the mount will fit close to the block and not leave any gaps.

It is now necessary to make the crown of the wig, either using wig net or a caul net. Turn the foundation net back from the galloon all round the inner edge of the mount; point the net in place and ease it into position; remove any points from underneath the wig net and replace them with points that are put in over the wig net and through the galloon.

Backstitch through the wig net and the galloon all round the inner edge of the mount. Trim off any surplus wig net and turn in the foundation net to the outer level of the galloon. Stitch through the two layers of net and the edge of the galloon in small neat stitches, thus holding the edge of the wig net firmly in place between the galloon and the foundation net [*Figure* 22(e)].

Finally, heat the pressing irons and carefully press all stitching on the mount by using the flat side of the iron and pressing over a piece of tissue paper.

SPRINGS

Wigs, transformations, and semi-transformations are held on the head by means of springs. Two kinds of springs are used: positional springs and tension springs. The positional springs are placed to hold the salient point down to the head, e.g., ear- and temple-peaks. The tension springs (see page 72) are placed at the back of the head on the galloon bind to tighten the postiche on the head and prevent it from slipping.

Positional springs

The positional springs must now be cut and covered. Nine springs are used for each wig mount and are placed in the following positions: two at each side, one from the ear-peak to the inner edge of the mount and one from the temple-peak to the inner edge and crossing on the bind as shown in *Figure* 22(f); one in the centre front; one on each side of the parting; and one on each side of the nape of the neck.

If the mount has no parting, the three springs at the centre front are arranged to fan out — one on each side of the centre spring. These springs are usually made of $\frac{3}{16}$ in. watch-spring but *can* be made of whalebone or piano-wire.

Measure and cut the springs carefully—very slightly less than the size they are required to be when finished. Rub the corners of the springs down on a stone to round them off and remove any sharp points [*Figure* 24(1*a*)].

Cover the top with a small piece of chamois leather glued into position. Trim off any surplus leather so that the ends will not be bulky [*Figure* 24 (1*b*)]. Take a small strip of fish-skin and wind this neatly over the tip to further secure the leather and prevent the spring from rubbing through the galloon. The fish-skin will stick easily if it is very slightly moistened.

The springs must now be covered with galloon so that they can be stitched into position on the mount. There are at least three different ways of covering springs but the simplest one is to cut a length of galloon just over twice the width and $\frac{1}{2}$ in. longer than the spring to be covered. Turn in $\frac{1}{4}$ in. of one end of the galloon and fold it in half lengthways. Put the spring inside this fold, stitch across the end, down the side, turn in

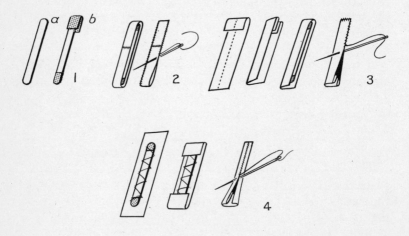

Figure 24. Covering positional springs

the other end and stitch across it [*Figure* 24(3)]; keep the stitches small and neat. Now the spring is ready for stitching in position. Alternatively a very narrow galloon may be used and stitched down on each side of the spring and across the centre (see *Figure* 24(2)].

Some wigmakers put the springs in position on the block, before putting on the net, so that they lie next to the head. In this case, to cover the spring they use the wider width of galloon, brace the spring in position in the centre of the galloon and seam the edges neatly down the top of the spring. This certainly makes a very neat job as no stitches are visible on the underside of the mount [*Figure* 24(4)].

When all the springs are covered, point them in position with block points putting one at each end of each spring. Sew the springs to the net down each side with a small hemming stitch, taking care to fasten the ends of the springs securely and removing the block points as the work proceeds. Press the sewing round the springs with heated pressing irons and the mount is ready for knotting.

TRANSFORMATIONS

Most of the instructions in the preceding section about making the wig mount apply equally to transformations and semi-transformations. There is no need therefore to repeat in exact detail the methods which occur again.

A transformation is like a wig without a crown but it has an opening at the centre back which fastens with a hook and eye. The wig mount is continuous round the hairline and has no opening. The pattern, however, is the same because a pattern is not normally cut for the crown of a wig.

Mounting

Place the pattern on the block using a block $\frac{1}{2}$ in. larger than the actual circumference measurement of the person for whom the transformation is intended. Using $\frac{1}{2}$ or $\frac{3}{4}$ centimetre galloon, point the bind ribbon in place, starting at the centre back, continuing round the front and finishing at the centre back. Cut off, leaving just enough galloon to turn over in a small hem at each side of the centre back [*Figure* 25(*a*)]. Sew

F

these tiny hems neatly, leaving a gap of $\frac{1}{4}$ in. between the two.

Outline the edge with $\frac{1}{4}$ or $\frac{1}{2}$ centimetre galloon all round the hairline edge, up the 1 in. depth of the mount at one side of the centre back, round the inner or crown edge of the mount and down the other side of the centre back [*Figure* 25(*b*)].

Make a neat join where the two ends of galloon meet and stitch neatly any small tucks at the corners of the centre back and ear-peaks. Point the foundation net in place, leaving the opening at the back.

Sewing

Sew down both edges of the bind and all round the inner edge of the galloon at the hairline, the inner edge of the crown and down the opening on each side of the centre back.

Brace as described for wigs round the hairline, taking care to brace to the galloon only. As there will be no crown of net to hold the inner edge in place, this too will require bracing. Place block points at $1\frac{1}{2}$ in. intervals and 1 in. from the edge all round the crown [*Figure* 25(*c*)].

Use strong white thread and brace tightly enough to hold the mount in position but not tightly enough to pull it out of shape. The two edges of the galloon at the centre back which are $\frac{1}{4}$ in. apart can be braced across to each other.

Trim off the foundation net, turn in and sew round the hairline, the crown edge, and each side of the centre back, so that all the edges are finished off neatly. Heat the pressing irons and press all sewing.

Springs

Cut and cover the positional springs in exactly the same way as for the springs of a wig mount using two extra ones — eleven springs in all [*Figure* 25(*d*)]. The two extra springs are placed one at each side of the centre-back opening. Point all the springs in place and sew, taking care not to break the net and to stitch the ends of the springs securely.

Remove all block points from the mount which should be

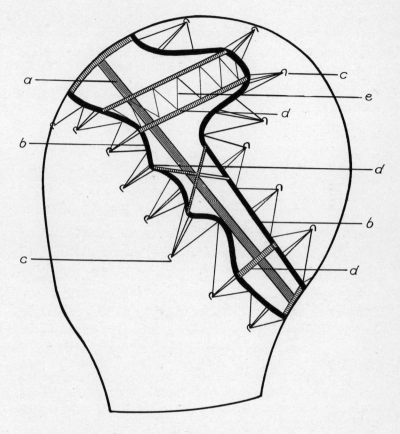

Figure 25. Transformation mount: (*a*) the galloon bind; (*b*) galloon at outer edge and round inner edge; (*c*) block points; (*d*) positional springs; (*e*) braced parting area.

held firmly in place by the bracing. Press the stitching on the springs and the mount is ready for knotting.

SEMI-TRANSFORMATIONS

The mount for a semi-transformation is very similar to the wig and transformation but it is a much smaller piece of postiche covering the front and sides of the head only.

Mounting the foundation

Place the pattern on the block in the position in which it is to be worn on the head. Point the galloon for the bind in place and leave enough extra length at each end to meet at the centre back, plus an extra 4 in. on each side for the tension springs to be inserted, as the semi-transformation is held in position by the tension springs which fasten at the centre back with a hook and eye [*Figure* 26(1*a*)]. Outline the edge of the mount with galloon all the way round both the hairline edge and the crown edge.

Point the foundation net in place with block points, remembering to take out any points in the bind before covering with net and replacing them with points on top of the net.

Sewing

Sew all round the bind taking care not to move its position and then sew all round the inner edge of the galloon which outlines the mount.

Brace all round, putting the looped points opposite the ear, temple-peaks and centre front and spacing the other points at equal intervals all round [*Figure* 26(2*b*)].

Finish off the outer edges by trimming off the foundation net, turning in to the level of the galloon edging and blanket-stitching finely. See details of sewing in *Figure* 30(2).

Springs

A semi-transformation needs 7 positional springs, one from each ear-peak to the inner edge of the mount and one from each temple-peak to the inner edge. These springs must cross

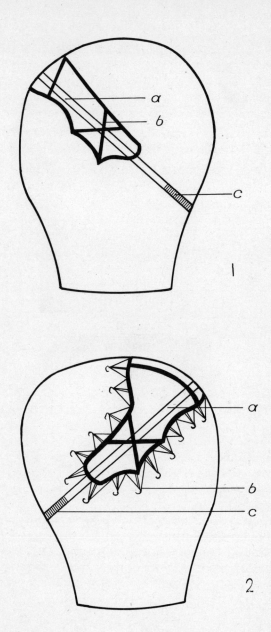

Figure 26. Semi-transformation mounts: 1(*a*) galloon bind; (*b*) positional springs; (*c*) tension spring. 2(*a*) galloon bind; (*b*) block points; (*c*) tension spring.

on the bind. The three springs at the centre front are arranged in a fan formation if there is no parting [*Figure* 26(1)].

Press all the sewing with heated pressing irons putting a piece of tissue paper between the net and the irons. The mount is now ready for knotting.

FOUNDATIONS WHICH INCLUDE A PARTING

Foundations for wigs, transformations, or semi-transformations sometimes include a parting. This is usually made by drawing the hair through fine flesh-coloured silk and it is termed a drawn-through parting (see page 94). It is made separately and inserted in the mount when completed.

The exact position, width, and length are allowed for: first, when cutting the pattern on which it must be clearly marked and, secondly, when mounting the foundation.

A parting is usually more than two inches in length, probably three or even four inches. Consequently the depth of the mount has to be extended at the position (left, right, or centre) in which the parting is to be inserted. This must be allowed for on the pattern and on the mount.

When outlining the mount with galloon it is not carried across the front edge of the parting. A positional spring is placed on each side of the parting extending from the hairline at the front to the crown edge of the mount. The foundation net is neatly turned in and sewn underneath this spring. After the springs are put on, the parting area should be braced across until the knotting of the mount is completed and the parting has been made and inserted. A careful study of *Figure* 25(*e*) shows how the bracing is done.

The reason for putting a spring on each side of the parting is not only to hold the edge down to the head, but also to prevent the parting itself from wrinkling, which it is inclined to do, particularly after it has been in wear for some time and has been cleaned.

TENSION SPRINGS

Wigs and transformations

Tension springs are used to tighten a wig or transformation on the head and are placed either at the centre back, or one on each side behind the ears. In either case they are placed on the underneath side of the foundation on the galloon bind, and are added after the knotting is completed.

Cut a piece of spring or elastic the required length [*Figure* 27(1)]. Stretch the spring and sew each end securely on the bind [*Figure* 27(2)]. Now sew another piece of galloon over the spring at each end and along each side so that the tension spring is held between the two layers of galloon and when the wig is taken off the block the spring will contract and tighten in the wig at the nape of the neck [*Figure* 27(3)].

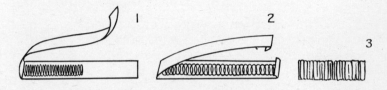

Figure 27. Making a tension spring

A transformation has tension springs inserted in the same way one at each side of the centre-back opening. A hook-and-eye is then stitched in place and the hook should be stitched facing outwards so that it does not cause discomfort in wear.

Semi-transformations and fringes

When a semi-transformation mount is made, the galloon bind should be left long enough to take the tension springs, one at each end [*Figure* 26(1) and (2)].

Sew the springs in the correct place at each end and stretch them to their full extent. Turn over the end of the galloon, which should be left long enough for this purpose, and sew along each side, so that the spring is held between the two layers of galloon [*Figure* 27(3)]. If springs are not available, a piece of narrow elastic can be stretched and sewn inside the galloon instead but it is not as durable as metal tension spring and is likely to require constant renewal.

A hook-and-eye is then sewn at the ends of the springs and the hook should be sewn turned outwards so that it does not press into the scalp and cause discomfort.

8 KNOTTING

SINGLE KNOTTING

Knotting is the means by which hair is implanted or fixed to the net foundation. A complete mastery of the art is necessary before knotting should be attempted on a foundation. There are three methods of knotting: single, double, and point knotting. The most commonly used is single knotting, so we will consider this first. A knotting hook is used and these are available in various thicknesses and are used according to the amount of hair required in the finished work [*Figure* 28].

Method: Pin a piece of stiff foundation net over a piece of paper on a malleable block. A paper of a contrasting colour to the net will be of help in seeing where to place the knots.

Put a quantity of hair in the drawing brushes with the root end protruding. Draw out a fine section of hair and turn over the root end about 1½ in. to form a loop. (It is possible to knot with much shorter roots when efficiency has been acquired.)

Hold this loop between the first finger and thumb in the left hand. Take the knotting hook in the right hand and hold it in the same way in which a pencil is held for writing. Insert it in one of the holes in the net and allow it to pass through and up at the next hole, so that one bar of net is held on the hook [*Figure* 28(1)].

Catch a few hairs from the loop of hair in the left hand and draw them through the net keeping them held on the hook [*Figure* 28(2)]. Turn the hook and catch the two ends of hair on it [*Figure* 28(3)] and draw them through the loop to form a knot [*Figure* 28(4)]. Tighten this knot, and draw the long ends right through so that they are firmly held on one bar of net [*Figure* 28(5)]. Considerable practice is necessary to achieve

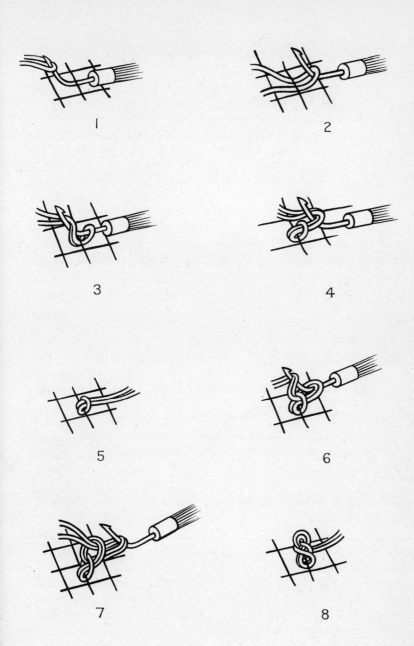

Figure 28. Single and double knotting

the required dexterity and to be able to place knots where required and falling in the right direction.

When the method of making single knots has been mastered a good way of learning how to 'place them' is to make a knotted parting. To do this, cut a pattern about 1 in. wide and 2 in. long in coloured paper. Pin it over a piece of brown paper on a malleable block and over this pin a piece of foundation net.

Take a needle threaded with white cotton and run a single thread along the centre of the parting. Run another thread across this one at right angles $\frac{1}{2}$ in. from the end of the pattern. Run two more threads diagonally from each corner of the parting, and number the sections as shown in *Figure* 29. Fill in each numbered section with single knots which should lie in the direction of the arrows on the diagram. All the sections at the crown should be filled in with a fine knot in every hole and in every row.

The sections numbered 1 and 5 can be knotted in every other hole and in every other row for the first three rows on each side. The remaining rows should be knotted in every hole and in every row up to the centre line.

When using stiffened foundation net, the direction in which the knots can be placed is limited by the structure of the net itself. If the knotting is done on knotting gauze, knots can be placed in any required direction and a more complicated crown arrangement is possible. This is one way of making a knotted parting but the more expensive ones are made on hair lace. It is intended here purely as an exercise in placing knots where required and in the correct thickness and direction.

DOUBLE KNOTTING

Double knotting is really an extension of single knotting and although rather unsightly, it is used on wig net or a caul net because it makes a more firmly held knot, which is necessary on the soft coarse net. This net is generally only used on the crown portion of a wig, so the knotting is not visible when the wig is finished.

Method: To make a double knot draw out a section of hair and turn over the root end to form a loop. Insert the hook

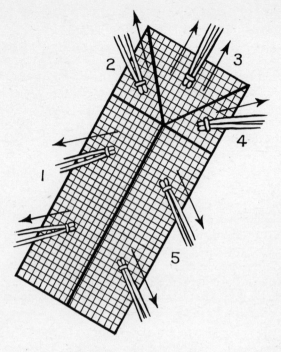

Figure 29. A knotted parting

through a bar of net and catch a few hairs from the loop of
hair in the left hand [*Figure* 28(1)]. Draw the hair through the
bar of net [*Figure* 28(2)], turn the hook and catch the long
ends [*Figure* 28(3)], and draw through the loop which is on
the hook [*Figure* 28(4)]. Instead of drawing the ends right
through, as for a single knot, tighten the knot, turn the hook,
catch the long ends again [*Figure* 28(6)] and draw through to
form a double knot [*Figure* 28(7)], drawing the long ends right
through the second loop [*Figure* 28(8)]. Tighten each knot as
it is made.

The net is much softer and has more 'give' than foundation
net. It, therefore, takes a little while to become used to knotting on it.

POINT KNOTTING

The actual knotting is done exactly as single knotting but in
such a way that only very short points of hair are left on the

foundation. It is used mainly in the making of men's postiche where the hair is required to be very short. It is not possible to knot hair in the normal way, leaving only 1 in. in length, without mixing up the roots and points, and this would not be satisfactory in wear. To achieve the effect of very short hair consisting of points only, point knotting is employed.

Method: Place the hair in the drawing brushes with the point end protruding instead of the roots. Draw off a section of hair and turn the point end over to make the loop. Turn over the length which is required for the finished work which may be anything from one to two inches. Make a row of ordinary single knots.

To remove the roots, back-comb the points right down to the foundation and cut the root ends off as close as possible without impairing the tightness of the knots. Comb out the remaining ends and they will give a very natural-looking short, wispy-haired effect. Point knotting may be used anywhere where this effect is required. In ladies' work it would be in the nape of a wig of short hair or for very light fringes, but it is used mainly for men's scalpettes or wigs.

KNOTTING OF WIGS, TRANSFORMATIONS, AND SEMI-TRANSFORMATIONS

All that part of the wig which is made of foundation net is done in single knotting. The extreme edge of the mount, all round the hairline is done first. These knots should be very fine and close together with no gaps in between and should lie in the natural direction of the hair growth.

The actual edge can be 'underdrawn', that is, by inserting the hook from the underneath side of the mount to the upper side so that the knot encloses the actual edge of the mount. If they are not done in this way, the hook should be placed from right to left on the left-hand side of the wig, and the opposite way on the right, so that the knots lie level and each knot should start where the previous one ends.

Two more rows should be knotted finely in every hole. The next $\frac{1}{2}$ in. should be knotted in every other hole and every other row and the remainder of the mount in every second hole and every second row. If the wig has a parting, all the right-hand side of the wig is knotted towards the right but slightly forwards and the left-hand side towards the left but also slightly forwards up to the parting area on each side.

If there is no parting, 2 in. in the centre front of the mount are cross-knotted; that is, one row to the right and the next row to the left, slightly forwards. This is done so that there will be no gap or break and the hair will stand up to a certain extent when combed back into a pompadour style.

All the foregoing applies to wigs, transformations and semi-transformations. But, in the case of a wig, there is the crown portion to fill in and as this is made of a caul or wig net it must be done in double knotting. The 2 in. at the centre back of the mount should be knotted either straight down, or cross-knotted in the same way as the centre front.

The double knotting on the crown portion should lie mainly towards the back of the head and should be spaced according to the amount of hair required. The knots should be closer together on the crown and top of the head than they are down in the nape, but the style of the wig will indicate where it is necessary to place the hair more thickly. Always try and follow the natural growth of the hair and remember that close, fine work will give a better effect than coarse work which is widely spaced. Pay special attention to the edges of hairwork because it is this part which is the most difficult to conceal.

UNDERKNOTTING

When all the knotting on the mount is completed, the bracing cotton should be cut and the mount taken off the block. Remove any surplus pieces of cotton and pin the wig or transformation wrong side up on a soft block.

Place one row of knotting all the way round the extreme edge of the mount facing in the same direction as the first row on the upper side. If some extra short hair is needed across the front, two or three rows of underknotting may be done, using short curled hair.

Heat the pressing irons and press all the knotting over a piece of tissue paper.

9 HAIR PIECES

THE CHIGNON

A chignon is a roll or bun of hair worn usually at the nape of the neck, but the term generally covers any added hair piece whether it is a cluster of curls, or a coil or plait worn on the back or crown of the head. It may be made of a switch, marteau, diamond mesh, or it may be knotted on a net foundation.

A knotted chignon is usually made of short curled hair and may be worn at the nape to hide shingled hair or on the crown to give height.

Pattern

It is necessary to measure the size of the mount required and to cut a pattern. Two pattern shapes are shown in *Figure* 30. A chignon mount for the nape [*Figure* 30(1)] would be about 4 in. to 5 in. long, and $1\frac{1}{2}$ in. to $2\frac{1}{2}$ in. wide at the centre, depending on the amount of hair required and the style in which it is to be dressed. When measuring the head, measure the circumference and use a block of the same size for mounting the pattern.

Mounting

Place the pattern on a block in the position in which it is intended to be worn. Outline the edge with $\frac{1}{4}$ or $\frac{1}{2}$ centimetre galloon; point this in position with block points, turning all the points outwards [*Figure* 30(2.2)]. Join the two ends of the galloon in a tiny run-and-fell seam. Point a piece of foundation net in place [*Figure* 30(2.3)].

Sewing

Sew all round the inner edge of the galloon, stitching through the net and the galloon [*Figure* 30(2.4)]. Trim off the net, leaving enough to turn in all round [*Figure* 30(2.5)].

Bracing

Put block points all the way round the mount about $1\frac{1}{2}$ in. apart and 1 in. from the outer edge. Turn each point over to form a small steel loop. Use white thread and brace to the galloon only all the way round following the method shown in *Figure* 23. Remove all the block points from the galloon edge as the work proceeds.

Finishing the mount

Trim off the surplus net [*Figure* 30(2.5)]. Turn in the edge of the foundation so that it is just level with the outer edge of the galloon [*Figure* 30(2.6)]. Sew through the edge of the net and the galloon in close small blanket-stitches all round and tighten in the edge as the work proceeds [*Figure* 30(2.7)].

Springs

It is not necessary to use springs on a very small mount but they may be included on a large one to hold it in shape. If used, they should be made of watch-spring, cut and covered in the usual way, one placed lengthways, and one across the centre of the mount. Stitch into position and then heat the pressing irons and press all the sewing.

Knotting

Use a fine knotting hook for the outer edge and knot all the way round in every hole for two rows. The extreme edge may be underdrawn by placing the hook in, from beneath the edge, and coming out on the top so that the knot encloses the actual edge of the mount.

The remainder of the mount should be knotted in every other hole and every other row, and a slightly thicker knotting hook may be used. If the mount is divided approximately

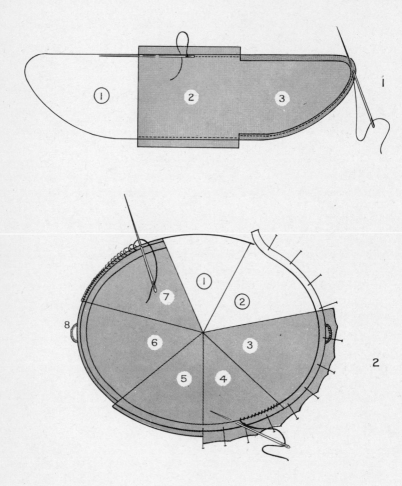

Figure 30. Patterns for chignons and sewing details for foundational postiche: (1) chignon pattern for the nape; (2) chignon pattern for the crown.

into three parts lengthways, the right-hand side should be knotted towards the right nape, and the left-hand side towards the left nape. The centre should then be knotted either straight down or crossknotted: that is, one row to the right and the following row to the left.

When all the net is filled in, cut the bracing cotton, take off the wooden block and pin the mount upside down on a malleable block. Using the fine hook, do one row of underknotting all round. Heat the pressing iron and press all the knotting over a piece of tissue paper.

Dressing

The chignon may be set and dressed out in any required style either as a cluster of curls or to look like a coil or roll of hair, always bearing in mind that it was designed to suit a particular dressing.

The chignon may be attached to the head either by a postiche comb placed in the centre of the mount or by two loops through which hairpins can be inserted [*Figure* 30(2.8)]. A chignon in the nape which has to be attached to comparatively short hair should have a small postiche clip at each side, or one postiche comb in the centre, and loops for pins at the side.

FRINGES OR FRONTS

A small fringe may be worn for various reasons — but it is used mainly when the hair is too thin to form the kind of dressing desired. It may be quite a small piece of postiche, or larger to cover a wider area in cases of loss of hair.

Cutting the pattern

The front edge is usually shaped to follow the hairline but it may be worn just a little further back so that the hair can combine with the wearer's own hair and this helps to give it a natural effect.

The usual length of the mount is from 4 in. to 6 in. and the depth from $1\frac{1}{2}$ in. to $2\frac{1}{2}$ in. or more, according to the area of scalp to be covered and the amount of hair to be used.

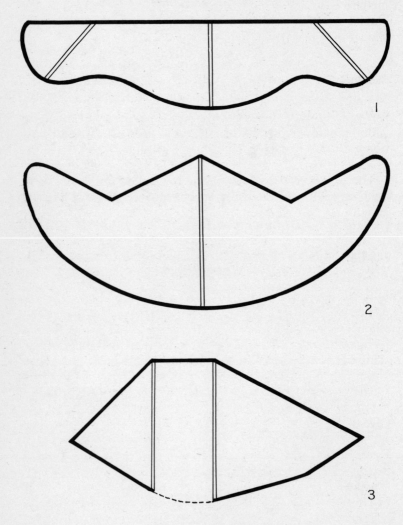

Figure 31. Fringe patterns

A typical pattern shape showing a mount 5 in. in length and 1½ in. deep at the centre front is shown in *Figure* 31(1). It may include a parting if required, in which case the mount would almost certainly be deeper. Alternative pattern shapes are shown in *Figure* 31(2) and (3).

Mounting

Mount the pattern on a wooden block in the position in which it is to be worn. Put a bind ribbon, using a ½ or ¾ centimetre galloon, in the usual position. This will strengthen the foundation and be of considerable help in attaching the fringe to the head.

The outer edge may be outlined in galloon or, if an extra light mount is required, this may be dispensed with and the edge finished in the way shown in *Figure* 30(1).

Sewing

Point the foundation net in place over the pattern. Sew the bind ribbon down each side. Take a length of silk and commence to sew at one end of the pattern. Make small running stitches exactly along the edge of the pattern, taking care not to break the net in sewing. Outline all round the pattern in small running stitches and tighten the edge in so that it fits closely to the block [*Figure* 30(1.2)].

The mount must now be braced. Put block points all round the mount, spacing them about 1½ in. apart and 1 in. from the edge of the mount. Be sure to place them so that one is opposite each main point of the mount and one opposite each end. Brace in the usual way but be careful not to sew over the net because this has to be trimmed off and turned over. Take the bracing stitches just round the outlining silk and the bar of net immediately adjoining it, or the net may easily break.

Trim off the net leaving about $\frac{3}{16}$ in. all round. Turn this over so that the running stitch forms the edge of the mount. Take another length of silk and make a second row of running stitches just inside the edge of the mount, sewing through both layers of net and again tightening-in any slackness at the edge [*Figure* 30(1.3)].

It is not usually necessary to put positional springs on a fringe mount unless it includes a parting, in which case one would be placed on each side of it to prevent the parting from wrinkling in wear. Press with heated pressing irons and the mount is ready for knotting.

Knotting

Single knotting is used all over. Knot the front edge first, finely in every hole for two rows. The centre two inches should be cross-knotted: that is, one row to the left and the next row to the right.

The next $\frac{1}{2}$ in. may be knotted in every other hole and in every row; also the remainder of the mount may be knotted in every other hole and every other row, keeping the work fine. The centre 2 in. should be cross-knotted all the way up and should be slightly thicker than the sides. When the knotting is completed, cut the bracing cotton and pin the mount inside out on a malleable block. Underknot all the front edge, one or two rows, as required.

In all knotting, use hair as far as possible in the length required for the finished work, so that very little trimming is needed. Finally, press all the work with heated pressing irons.

If the fringe is to be kept on the head by tension springs in the galloon bind, make these and insert them at this stage. It can be secured by clips or by a postiche comb in the centre and clips at the ends. The method of securing depends largely on the amount of hair of the wearer.

Dressing

Pin the mount right side up and set in the required style. Dry in the postiche oven and then dress out ready for wear.

POSTICHE COMBS

One of the most useful ways of attaching small pieces of postiche to the hair is by the use of a postiche comb. These are available in various sizes and are similar to side combs. They must be attached to the piece of postiche and to do this, it is necessary to cover the top of the comb with galloon so that it can be sewn to the foundation.

Method: Cut a piece of galloon ½ in. larger than the top of the comb, and twice as wide. Make a small seam at each side and turn right-side out. The galloon then forms a little cap which will fit over the top of the comb [*Figure* 32(1)]. Take a fine needle and thread, and stitch the edges of the galloon together between each tooth of the comb so that it is held firmly and neatly in position over the top of the comb [*Figure* 32(2)]. The top edge of the galloon can now be sewn where required to the piece of postiche.

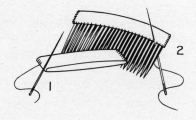

Figure 32. Covering a postiche comb: (1) cap made of galloon; (2) cap fitted over top of comb and stitched between each tooth.

A large-sized comb is useful for attaching a marteau to form a chignon. It should be stitched to the top of the marteau and is almost invisible in wear. A medium-sized comb can be used to hold a small fringe in place or for a curled chignon on the crown. The method of covering the top of the comb is the same in each case. Use galloon to match the colour of the hair.

MEN'S POSTICHE

When making men's postiche it is essential to have a foundation which fits perfectly because there is so very little hair to hide any defects. If, therefore, a man has a head of an unusual shape it is advisable to make a plaster cast so that the postiche can be made on an exact replica of the wearer's head, thus ensuring a perfect fit. The exact method of making a plaster cast is described in *The Art and Craft of Hairdressing** to which reference should be made. For all normal purposes a block of the correct size is adequate.

SCALPETTES

A scalpette is more often made for men than for women because it is unusual for a woman to be affected with loss of hair in a patch in the same way as a man. It covers all the portion of the head which has gone bald on the top but is not so extensive as a complete wig. If a man becomes completely bald and has to wear a wig it is very difficult to disguise the edges owing to the present fashion for short hair. A scalpette is much more adaptable because the hair combs in with the wearer's own hair and can blend in almost invisibly.

Cutting the pattern

The scalpette itself is irregular in shape and the pattern should be cut and fitted on the person for whom it is intended. Measure from the centre-front hairline on the forehead to the furthest back point affected by loss of hair [*Figure* 33(1)]. Then take a series of cross-measurements at 2 in. intervals to ascertain the exact width at different points of the bald patch [*Figure* 33(2)]. Draw these in on a piece of paper, and cut out the approximate shape of the patch [*Figure* 33].

Moisten the paper slightly and press it down on the scalp, easing-in the edges. Take a pair of scissors and trim off just inside the hairline all round the sides and back. The front hairline will have to be estimated but there are usually one or two hairs growing along the hairline even in the most extreme cases of baldness. If these are not present it may be possible to study a photograph taken at an earlier date and estimate the hairline.

Before taking the pattern from the head, strengthen the edges by rounding off with gummed paper or sellotape. When the pattern is removed, it will show the exact shape and contours of the head, and a suitable block will have to be

---

* Wolters, N. E. B., (London: The New Era Publishing Co., 4th ed. 1958.)

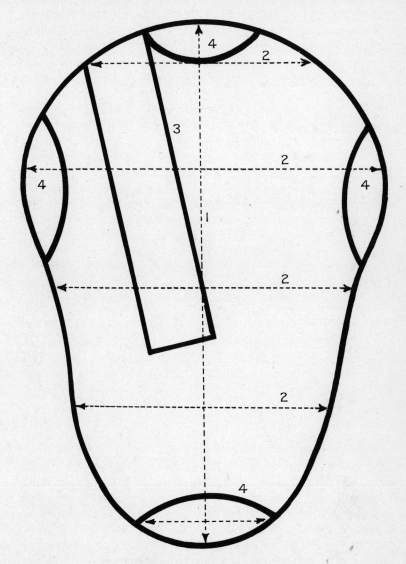

Figure 33. Scalpette pattern

chosen on which to make the foundation. It is necessary to measure the circumference of the head as a guide to the size of block required. If a parting is to be included, pencil the exact position on the pattern while it is still on the head [*Figure* 33(3)].

A scalpette is held in position on the head by means of adhesive patches, usually 4 or 6 depending on the size and shape of the foundation. These are placed at the salient points and outlined with galloon to give added strength. Their position is indicated in *Figure* 33(4).

Mounting the foundation

Choose a wooden block of the same circumference as the head and as near in shape as possible. Place the pattern on the block with one or two block points to hold it in place. Be sure to put it in the exact position in which the scalpette is to be worn. The places for adhesive patches should be marked on the pattern. Using $\frac{1}{4}$ or $\frac{1}{2}$ centimetre galloon, outline the inner edge of each adhesive place and cut off the galloon at the hairline edge on each. Turn the block points in towards the crown. Outline all the outer edge of the scalpette with the same width of galloon but this time turn all the block points outwards. Make the join at the centre back and cut off, leaving enough galloon to make a tiny seam.

Sewing

Neatly sew all the joins in the galloon, and there will be one at each side of each adhesive point. Heat the pressing irons and press each sewn point, removing any block points which are not necessary.

Cover the entire mount either with stiffened foundation net or with knotting gauze. It will need considerable easing-in at the edges if the mount is fairly extensive and it may help if the net is slightly moistened. Use only a minimum of block points because all the block points which are holding the galloon, outlining the adhesive points on the inside of the mount, have to be removed as the sewing proceeds so that no block points are left underneath the net. Sew all round both sides of these inner pieces of galloon, removing the block points and readjusting the net as the work proceeds.

Then sew all around the inner edge of the galloon which outlines the foundation. Trim off the net or gauze leaving just over $\frac{1}{8}$ in. all round for turning in.

Bracing

Turn the net back from the edge, so that it will be easy to brace to the galloon only. Place block points opposite each of the salient points and at evenly spaced intervals in between, about 1 in. from the edge of the mount and $1\frac{1}{2}$ in. apart, turning each point over to make a small steel loop. Using white cotton, brace in the way which has been previously described [*Figure* 23]. The bracing must be tight enough to hold the mount firmly but not so tight that the edge is pulled out of shape. Use fairly strong white cotton and remove all the block points from the galloon edge as the bracing proceeds.

Sew all round the outer edge of the mount by turning in the edge of the net so that it is just level with the edge of the galloon; use blanket-stitching all round. Tighten-in the edge so that it lies close to the block and will thus fit close to the scalp.

It is not usual to use springs on a scalpette unless a drawn through parting is included, in which case one would be placed on each side of the parting, mainly to prevent it from wrinkling and becoming unsightly in wear. When the sewing is completed, heat the pressing irons and press all sewing over a piece of tissue paper.

Knotting

For a man's scalpette, hair must be chosen with extra care because it has to comb in with the wearer's own hair which may be a completely different shade on the temples, if it is going grey, than at the back of the head. It is important therefore to bear this point in mind and, if necessary, to take two or even three patterns of hair.

Most of the knotting is done in single knotting, but it is often advisable to use point knotting at the edges of the mount, particularly on the temples and where the hair has to be worn very short at the back. This is done so that the root end of the hair can be cut out close to the foundation and points of hair of only $\frac{1}{2}$ in. to $1\frac{1}{2}$ in. in length can be left; this would not be possible using the common method of single knotting.

Knot all round the edge of the foundation first; commence 1 in. to the right at the back edge and place the knots close together. Put the hook in from right to left so that the knots lie to the right and make them so close that the hook goes in for each successive knot where it came out in the previous knot, leaving no gap between knots. Use a fine hook and do all the outer edge in point knotting. Continue in the same direction until 1 in. past the centre front.

Start again at the back, 1 in. to the left of the centre, and place the knots close together as before, but this time, lying in the opposite way so that the 2 in. at the centre back and 2 in. at the centre front are cross-knotted: that is, one row to the right and one row to the left. Fill in the remainder of the mount, make the knots fall in the direction of the natural hair-growth but space them much further apart. If a very fine hook is used, they may be spaced in every other hole, and in every other row. If a coarser hook is used, they may be further apart still, except for $\frac{1}{2}$ in. from the front hairline. For this use a fine hook and place the knots in every hole for the first two rows; subsequent rows should be knotted in every other hole but the work must be fine when done so closely together. If there is no parting, the centre 2 in. should be cross-knotted. This will prevent a gap in the hair which would show the foundation.

By carefully grading the lengths of hair used, it should be possible to obviate an undue amount of trimming to the finished work which will help to give it a natural appearance. The hair on the top of the head will of course be longer than the hair at the sides and point knotting should be continued until it has reached a length at which the desired effect can be achieved by ordinary single knotting.

Underknotting

When all the net is filled in, take the mount off the block by cutting the bracing cotton and pulling out any loose bits of thread. Remove the pattern and pin the mount inside out on a malleable block.

Put one row of underknotting all the way round the mount, using point knotting and following the direction of the hair on the upper side of the mount. Use a very fine hook and leave no gaps between the knots. Heat the pressing irons, put a piece of tissue paper over the knotting and press all round the edge and the under-side of the mount, thus pressing all the knotting.

Adhesive points

It is necessary to sew a small piece of oiled silk on each of the places outlined with galloon and intended for use as adhesive points. This should be done as neatly as possible, particularly at the front edge, avoiding any bulkiness.

The oiled silk prevents any stickiness, which may come from the adhesive used to hold the scalpette in position, from penetrating the foundation and the hair. The adhesive may be spirit gum, or, preferably, toupée adhesive which is similar to adhesive plaster but sticky on both sides so that one side sticks to the scalp and the other to the oiled silk.

Dressing

Take the scalpette off the block, turn it over and pin it on a malleable block in the position in which it will be worn. Set it in any desired style and dress out. Some trimming may be necessary but this may be left and done on the head of the wearer.

10 DRAWN-THROUGH PARTINGS

Most partings for modern wigs are made by knotting the hair on gauze or net and afterwards drawing through fine flesh-coloured silk. The parting may be of any length or width (as required) and its position and size must be clearly marked on the pattern, and a space prepared for it on the mount. The parting is usually made separately and inserted in the parting space on completion. Any gaps on the parting silk or round the edges may be filled in with single knotting after the insertion of the parting.

ENGLISH METHOD

Cut a pattern to the exact size of the parting space and mark the front clearly. Shape the front edge to fit in with the rest of the mount. Pin the pattern on a malleable block, over a piece of folded paper of a contrasting colour, with a single pin through the centre front. Pin a piece of gauze or foundation net, at least $\frac{1}{2}$ in. bigger all round than the pattern, over it.

Knotting

Use single knotting and place the knots so that they lie straight forward. Commence about $\frac{1}{2}$ in. from the front edge, more or less according to the length of parting. If ordinary foundation net is used, the knotting should be done finely in every hole and every row. But if gauze is used, knot in every hole and every other row.

The roots should be kept short and level while knotting and must be back-combed and cut out every two or three rows. They should be cut as close as possible to the foundation without damaging or loosening the knots. This is done so that no unsightly short ends will be drawn through the silk. Fill up the whole pattern in this way. The last few rows may be done slightly thicker to avoid a bare appearance at the end of the parting. Follow the pattern exactly except for the spare $\frac{1}{2}$ in. allowed at the front.

Drawing-through

When the knotting is completed and all the roots are cut out, comb all the hair smoothly towards the front. A drop of brilliantine on the hair will facilitate the drawing-through process. Pin a piece of parting-silk over the whole area. This piece of silk may be 1 in. more than the actual pattern all round to allow room to pin it and adjust it as the drawing-through progresses.

Use a very fine gauze hook and commence to draw the hair through at the back edge. The first $\frac{1}{2}$ in. should be slightly thicker than the remainder of the parting. It is advisable to start just below the last row of knotting so that the hook does not catch in the knots and pull them undone. The silk should be pinned quite taut as it is easier for the hook to penetrate in this way, and it should be adjusted to keep it so, as the work proceeds.

Hold the hook almost perpendicular and insert it through the silk to catch one or two hairs. It is not necessary to draw the hairs right out at each insertion; they can be held on the hook until half an inch or more has been completed. Then draw them right out in as upright a position as possible. Work in complete rows and space the insertions approximately over the knots underneath.

Considerable practice is required both in spacing the insertions and in penetrating far enough to pick up the hair but not to catch the knots or tear the parting-silk. If the silk does inadvertantly become torn, it can easily be pulled off and replaced with a new piece. Comb the hair smoothly again before pinning on the new silk, and draw-through afresh.

Keep to the edges of the pattern and work right down to the front edge. There will be enough hair, even though the knotting commenced half an inch back. Draw the last two rows slightly closer together.

When all the hair is drawn-through, or the front edge is reached, take the parting off the block. Trim the foundation net or gauze close to the knotting down each side and level with the pattern at the front edge. Cut out any surplus hair which has not been drawn through. Turn the parting silk over in a small neat hem and sew all round. Press the edges with pressing irons.

Inserting

Fix the parting in position on the mount with block points and sew in neatly along each side with fine running stitches. Fill in any gaps down the sides in single knotting which should lie straight forward. Use the fine gauze hook to fill in the small space at the back of the parting. Knot close together in rows, one row to the right and the following row to the left until the space is filled.

The parting may now be combed and the hair parted where required. The hair should stand up and appear to be growing in a natural way. No knotting or net should be visible in the parting area.

FRENCH METHOD

In the French method, knotting and drawing through are completed in one operation.

Prepare the pattern and net or gauze as before. Cut the parting silk and pin at the front edge only. Knot the hair to the gauze or net by inserting the hook through the parting silk and holding the hair between the net and the silk. The hair is then knotted to the net and drawn through the silk in one operation. The net, clearly visible through the parting silk, guides the placing of the hook. The silk can be pinned down as the work advances.

When the whole area is filled in, the parting is finished off as before by trimming off the surplus net or gauze and turning the silk over in a small neat hem ready for inserting in the mount.

The original French technique, brought to England about 140 years ago, is practised only by very experienced craftsmen. The English method developed from it, and suited less experienced postiche-makers. It is the method mostly used today.

11 MAINTENANCE OF POSTICHE

CLEANING AND DRESSING POSTICHE

It is not advisable to clean finished postiche by washing in soap and water. In the case of foundational postiche it would cause the knots to become loose and thus cause the hair to come out. It would also shrink the foundation net and make the postiche go out of shape. Much the same applies to postiche made of weft. Soap and water causes the weaving to become loose and eventually come undone. Therefore, some other fluid must be used for cleaning. There are three possible cleaning fluids, each of which has its advantages and disadvantages. They are: white petrol, industrial spirit, and carbon-tetrachloride.

White petrol is reasonably efficient as regards cleansing. It is also comparatively inexpensive, but it is, however, highly inflammable and should never be used near a naked flame. It is also inclined to leave rather an unpleasant odour in the hair, even after several hours have been allowed for evaporation. Industrial spirit will also remove all grease and dirt but it, too, is inflammable. The customs and excise regulations controlling its sale and use are a further discouragement.

Nowadays, there are several proprietary brands of cleaning fluid, made mainly of carbon-tetrachloride, which are the most suitable. They are efficient and non-inflammable. Their only disadvantage is that they make one feel sleepy if used in a confined space; therefore, always use these cleaning fluids in a room with a good current of air going through it, or in the open air.

To clean a wig or other postiche

Comb out the postiche carefully, working from the points first. Take care not to catch the teeth of the comb in the net foundation. Never use a brush on the actual foundation as it loosens the knots. Examine the foundation and if any repairs are required, attend to them before cleaning. Any small hole or tear in the net, can be neatly darned. Tension springs may need to be renewed or positional springs replaced.

Pour out enough cleaning fluid into a bowl to cover the wig completely. Fold the wig into a small compass and immerse in the fluid. Allow it to stand for a minute of two to loosen the grease, then work the fluid through the hair; let it run from roots to points until the dirt and grease come away.

If the fluid gets very dirty, it may be necessary to repeat the process with another bowl of clean fluid. Pay particular attention to the foundation which collects grease and take care not to be rough when handling the parting.

When it is clean, gently squeeze out all the surplus moisture; shake it well, but gently, in the open air and hang it out to allow all the fluid to evaporate.

A wig can be carefully pegged to the clothes line out of doors by means of a spring-type of clip but peg it at the nape of the neck: always hang it out by its strongest part and do not allow any strain to fall on the foundation.

When all the fluid has evaporated (this usually takes several hours), bring the wig indoors and pin it carefully on a malleable block of the correct size. Place one pin at each ear-peak, one at the centre front and one at each side of the nape. Always follow this rule for it is much easier to remove the wig from the block when it is finished without disturbing the dressing because you know exactly where it is pinned down. Comb out all the tangles carefully and the wig is ready for setting.

Place a can of hot water on the work-bench near you. Thoroughly wet the hair by dipping the comb in the water and shaking it on the wig as you comb it out. Do not put the wig under the tap, or cause the foundation to become any wetter than is absolutely necessary. In particular, try not to saturate the silk of a drawn-through parting.

When setting a wig in waves, hold these in position by

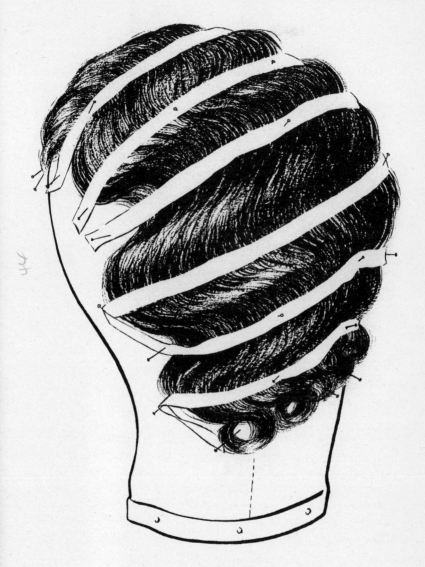

Figure 34. Semi-transformation in *First pli*

pinning tapes along each wave [see *Figure* 34]. There is usually some short hair in front and this should be set in small pin-curls which are held in position by two ordinary pins placed through each curl and into the block. Never put hairpins or other clips through the foundation net as it is easily torn. Use only steel pins of the same quality as those used by dress-makers. Loose curls can be made either over rollers or cotton wool. The first setting of the wig is called putting the wig in *First pli*.

Put a net over the waves or curls and place in a warm postiche oven to dry. This may take an hour or several hours, according to the type of postiche oven employed. Some of the modern electric ovens have a mild current of air as well as heat and these are quicker than the ones with heat alone.

When the hair and foundation are quite dry, take out of the oven, remove the net and all the pins, tapes, curlers or whatever has been used for setting. Comb the hair through and arrange it in the way it is intended to be worn. Back comb if necessary but do not back comb close to the foundation as it is sometimes difficult to comb out and shortens the life of a wig considerably.

Put the net back loosely over the set and put the wig back in the postiche oven to set the style. The wig is now in *Second pli*.

Leave for 20 to 30 minutes, bring out of the oven, make any final adjustments to the style. If the hair is dry, a little bril-liantine may be sprayed on or a light spray of hair lacquer may be used. Do not use too much. The wig is now ready for placing on the client and is said to be in *Third pli*.

If it has to be packed and sent away or stored, take the pins out and carefully take the wig off the block. Place a wad of tissue paper underneath and inside the crown to hold it in place. Lower it gently into a postiche box, ready prepared with two pieces of tissue paper. Fold these over the wig and store until required.

Special precautions when cleaning and dressing white hair

If the foregoing process is being done on white hair, every care must be taken to prevent discoloration:

1 Be sure that all tools, blocks, etc., are scrupulously clean, especially during the setting and dressing out operation.
2 A little blue rinse may be added to the water used for setting.
3 Before putting the wig in the oven to dry, pin a piece of tissue paper over it for added protection.
4 Do not have the postiche oven too hot.

Most of these points would also apply when attending to a client with white hair.

General advice to postiche clients

If a wig is worn regularly it is advisable to have at least two, and preferably three. Not only because one wig can be cleaned while the other is in use, but so that they can be worn on alternate days and thus be given an opportunity to air.

Have the wig professionally cleaned and have it done at frequent and regular intervals. The reason for this is to keep the wig looking attractive and to prolong its life. If grease is allowed to accumulate on the foundation, it will cause it to rot and tear quickly.

Advise the client to keep her own hair short if possible and to keep it clean by regular shampooing, or the grease will come through on to the wig. Also, an unwashed head and scalp may become unhealthy.

Handle a wig carefully at all times. Show the client the easiest way to put it on: from the front and always ensure that the centre front is correctly placed, then ease it down towards the back. Arrange the hair to suit the face and never comb roughly by allowing the teeth of the comb to catch in the foundation net.

Finally, advise the client never to wash the wig in soap and water because it would cause the foundation to shrink and loosen the knotting. Expert advice should be sought if any alteration in size, or any repairs, are required.

MISFITS

It sometimes happens that in spite of careful measuring a wig may be too tight or too slack, or it might be the intention of the wearer to use a wig which was not originally made for his or her use.

If there is much variation in the measurement from ear to ear across the front it is not a practicable job to alter the wig. If, however, it is a matter of half to one inch and the adjustment can be made on the portion of the wig behind the ears, it is possible to make a satisfactory alteration.

To make a wig smaller

A small degree of slackness can be taken up by adjusting the tension springs. If more than half an inch must be taken in, it will be necessary to make a small tuck in the foundation. This will need to be made in the mount only as the caul net is easy to adjust without stitching into a tuck. The most convenient place to make it is at the centre back, and not behind the ears because here the wig requires two tucks, one at each side, or the wig would be thrown out of balance.

Take off the tension spring. Decide on the exact size and position of the tuck required then carefully cut off the hair from this part of the mount, close to the foundation. If it is left in the tuck, it makes unnecessary bulk. Make the tuck, sewing the extra net on the under side of the mount and try to avoid any lumpiness in the sewing. Press carefully and replace the tension springs or spring.

To make a wig larger

Unless more than half an inch is required the simplest way is to make the alteration at the centre back. If, however, the alteration is more and it is decided to make it behind the ears, this is done in exactly the same way. As the alteration must be made behind each ear, half the amount must be added on each side.

Take off the tension spring. Cut off any hair which is over the portion of net involved in the sewing. Make a clean cut right through the edge of the mount, net, bind ribbon and inner edge of the mount. Join in the required amount of net, galloon edging and bind. Be very careful not to make any lumpy joins because any unevenness in the mount can cause extreme discomfort and irritation to the wearer, particularly if done behind the ears. When the sewing is completed, heat the pressing irons, press well and replace the tension spring.

Turn the wig over and pin on a malleable block. Knot in hair to match, on the extra piece of foundation net, following the direction and thickness of the previous knotting. Press the knotting and finally put the wig in *pli* and dress out when dry.

Glossary

ADHESIVE PATCH: A small area on the underside of men's postiche which is covered with oiled-silk.

BEESWAX: The prepared secretion of the bee, used for strengthening sewing and weaving silk.

BIGOUDI: A small wooden curler on which the hair is wound for permanently curling.

BIND: A piece of galloon which is attached to the underside of the wig, encircling the head.

BOARDWORKER: One who makes postiche.

BOX-IRON: An obsolete type of crimping iron.

BRACING: The cottons which hold the foundation in position on the wooden block during the process of knotting.

CACHE PEIGNE: A covered comb which may be used for attaching a chignon to the hair.

CHIGNON: A small piece of woven or knotted postiche, worn between the crown and nape of the neck, to elaborate the finished dressing.

CRÊPE-HAIR: Human hair which has been permanently crimped by weaving, boiling, and baking.

CRÉPON: A frontlet extended in length to the top of the ears, and dressed in pompadour style.

CROQUIGNOLE: Winding from point to root.

DIAMOND MESH: A method of sewing up weft into diamond-shaped meshes. The weaving incorporates one strand of wire.

DOUBLE-ADHESIVE PLASTER: Plaster which is adhesive on both sides, used on the adhesive patch.

DOUBLE KNOTTING: The means of attaching hair to wig or caul net.

DRAWN-THROUGH PARTING: A specially prepared portion of a wig in which the hair, after being knotted, is drawn-through a very fine strong silk material, which gives the appearance of the natural scalp.

FELTING:
The manner in which the root ends of the hair adhere together after being rubbed on the palm of one hand, thus eliminating tying when preparing permanently curled hair.

FINISHING-KNOT:
The manner of weaving the final strand of hair to prevent the work from becoming loose.

FLAT WEFT:
Once-in weaving.

FLY WEFT:
Fine weaving used for the top-row of postiche made of weft.

FOUNDATION:
The base of any piece of postiche made of net (including wig net), to which the hair is attached.

FRINGE:
A small piece of frontal postiche.

FRISURE FORCÉE:
A method of permanently curling hair used in postiche.

HACKLING:
A process by which tangled hair may be disentangled.

HAIR-LACE:
A form of net foundation made of stiffened human hair.

HANK:
Sewing or weaving silk may be supplied in this form by the manufacturers.

MARTEAU(X):
Postiche made of weft sewn flat and finished with loops or mounted on a postiche clip or comb.

MIXING:
The intermingling of hair of various shades and (or) lengths.

MOUNT:
That part of a wig (excluding the crown), transformation, semi-transformation, or smaller piece of postiche made of foundation net, hair-lace, or gauze, on which the hair is knotted.

OILED-SILK: Used to protect those areas of men's postiche where an adhesive is placed.

PAPILLOTE CURLING: The method of curling using triangular pieces of paper and heated pinching irons.

PARTING-SILK: Fine strong silk used for making drawn-through partings.

PERIWIG: An old-fashioned name for a wig.

PERUKE: Another old-fashioned name for a wig.

PERUQUIER: A wigmaker.

PLI: The manner in which the hair is set prior to dressing out.

POINT KNOTTING: A method of knotting which ensures that only the points of the hair remain as part of the finished work.

POSTICHE CLIP: A specially devised clip for attaching small pieces of hair-work to the hair.

POSTICHE OVEN: An oven which emits a gentle heat similar to an everyday drying cabinet.

POSTICHEUR: One who designs and dresses postiche.

SCALPETTE: A piece of postiche worn by men to cover an irregularly shaped bald area on the front and (or) crown of the head.

SEMI-TRANSFORMATION: Frontal postiche extending to just above or behind the ear.

SPRINGS: Used in order to retain the shape and position of foundational postiche on the head.

STARTING-KNOT: The manner of weaving the first strand of hair.

STOP BLOCKS: Wooden blocks attached to the work-bench to prevent the hackle or brushes from slipping.

STRINGS: The term used when referring to the silks on the weaving frame.

SWATHE: Knotted or woven postiche usually worn at the nape of the neck.

SWITCH: Woven postiche with one, two or three stems.

TEASING: The preliminary, manual loosening of en-
                    tangled hair prior to hackling.

TORSADE: Woven or foundational postiche, dressed
                    in a variation of coils and curls.

TOUPÉE: A man's semi-wig, rather larger than a
                    scalpette.

TOUPET: A lady's frontal postiche, larger than a
                    fringe but not so large as a semi-trans-
                    formation.

TRANSFORMATION: Foundational postiche consisting of a
                    knotted mount which completely encircles
                    the hairline.

TURNING: The process by which hair cuttings or
                    combings are arranged so that all the root
                    ends are together.

TWICE-IN WEFT: A more widely spaced method of weaving
                    than once-in weaving.

UNDERKNOTTING: Fine knotting used under the hair-line of
                    foundational postiche.

WATCH-SPRING: Metal spring similar to that used in watch-
                    making: it is used in wigmaking for the
                    purpose of ensuring that the foundation
                    fits comfortably on the head.

WEFT-WIG: A wig in which the attached hair is woven
                    instead of knotted.

WIG-WEFT: Another name for thrice-in weaving, also
                    known as 'crop'.

Index